THE SANE ALTERNATIVE

A Choice of Futures

James Robertson

Revised and Expanded Edition, 1983

First published 1978
Reprinted 1978
Revised edition 1983

ISBN 0 9505962 1 3

United States editions, 1979, 1980: River Basin Publishing Co.,
Box 30573, St. Paul, Minnesota 55175, U.S.A.

German edition, Die lebenswerte Alternative, 1979:
Fischer Taschenbuch Verlag, Frankfurt, Germany.

Swedish edition, Det sunda alternativet, 1981:
Liber Forlag, Stockholm, Sweden.

Revised edition printed and bound in Great Britain
by Gibbons Barford Print, Wolverhampton.

Copies can be obtained from James Robertson, Spring Cottage,
9 New Road, Ironbridge, Shropshire TF8 7AU.

ABOUT THE AUTHOR

James Robertson believes that industrialised societies and the world as a whole are now at a turning point; the 'post-industrial revolution' has begun.

Since 1973 he has worked as an independent writer, speaker and adviser. From their cottage in Ironbridge, Shropshire, he and his wife, Alison Pritchard, keep in touch through the Turning Point network with other people in many parts of the world who feel that new values, new lifestyles and a new system of society must be helped to break through, as the old ones continue to break down.

Robertson's early career — from 1953 to 1965 — was in government. He served in the British Cabinet Office, and in 1960 he accompanied Prime Minister Harold Macmillan on the 'wind of change' tour of Africa. Subsequently, after some years' experience in systems analysis and management consulting, Robertson set up the Inter-Bank Research Organisation and directed it for the British banks from 1968 until 1973.

Between 1965 and 1973 he was involved in many enquiries and studies on the organisation of Britain's government, civil service, and Parliament; on relations between government and industry; and on the future role of London as a world financial centre.

James Robertson's other books are: 'The Reform Of British Central Government' (1971); 'Profit Or People? The New Social Role Of Money' (1974); and 'Power, Money And Sex: Towards A New Social Balance' (1976).

CONTENTS

INTRODUCTION

More and more people believe that the human race must break through to a new kind of future. Failure will mean disaster; success will mean an important upward step on the ladder of evolutionary progress. Many of us see this breakthrough as the central project, the historic task, for the two or three generations living at the present time — the task which gives meaning to our lives. Some of us sense that a threefold era is now ending: first, the age which began with the industrial revolution two hundred years ago; second, the age of European ascendancy which began with the Renaissance and Reformation five hundred years ago; and, third, the age of the successor civilisations to Athens, Jerusalem, and Rome which began roughly with the birth of Christ two thousand years ago. This suggests a historical perspective, and a measure of our task as midwives to a new future.

I first became aware of the need for this book in the mid-1970s, while talking about present problems and future possibilities with people in Britain, Europe and North America. A clear discussion document was needed, reasonably short, which would suggest:

what a sane, humane, ecological future will be like, as contrasted with other possible visions of the future;

by what kind of process that future can be created;

what kind of activities will contribute to bringing it about.

Since the first edition of 'The Sane Alternative'[1] came out five years ago, recognition that humankind is at a turning point has become much more widespread. Many people now see the 1980s as a critical decade. The 1960s were a time of naive optimism, both on the part of technocrats assuming that their managerialist approach could create a better future, and on the part of students and other young people who hoped that the counterculture would transform society in a short space of time. The 1970s were a decade of disappointment and stagnation; the naive hopes of both sides had to be reappraised. Now the 1980s seem to present a clear choice. Either we face breakdown — a destructive polarisation of social forces in which the two sides react against each other into ever greater extremism. Or we break through to a new direction of development in which managerial competence and technological knowhow play their necessary, but subordinate, part in creating a future in which people matter.

As I explained in the introduction to the first edition, my wife (Alison Pritchard) and I published it ourselves, as a practical experiment in self-reliance in keeping with the general message of the book. We hoped that self-publication would make it easier to encourage use of the book as discussion material and to assess its practical usefulness for that purpose. Also, by enabling us to be in touch personally with people who found the book useful, we hoped that self-publication would link it in with other aspects of our work, including the Turning Point network.[2] In these ways we hoped in due course to be able to revise the book in response to suggestions from readers.

The experiment proved successful. Our own edition had to be reprinted, and editions have also been published in the United States, Germany and Sweden.[3] In other countries, too, 'The Sane Alternative' has achieved recognition and has been well received. It clearly meets a need.

As I hoped, three main types of reader have found the book useful.

First, there are people who know that a new direction is necessary and possible for the future, and want to help to steer things in that direction. It has been good to know from many letters and discussions that 'The Sane Alternative' has been helpful and encouraging to such people, and to have received so many constructive comments and suggestions from them.

Second, there are people who, even if they do not share my perspective, have a professional interest in possibilities for the future. I mean people like industrial leaders, business managers, politicians, bankers, public administrators, personnel managers, trade unionists, academics, and members of professions like medicine, teaching and social work. Their activities will be profoundly affected by how the future evolves. They will need to adapt. They know they cannot ignore the growing number of people who now want a sane, humane, ecological future. Increasingly, they are, in fact, studying what such a future will involve. It has been good to know that for quite a number of them 'The Sane Alternative' has helped to confirm that the vision of the future which it outlines may be less utopian and more realistic

7

— more feasible — than conventional thinking used to suggest.

Third, there are people who, without yet being deeply involved or professionally interested in the future, are beginning to think seriously about it. It has been good to hear from many such individuals and groups that the book has helped them to clarify their ideas on the future, and to get more deeply involved in it themselves.

For us, personally, 'The Sane Alternative' has provided a foundation for our work during the last five years. This has included a short university attachment to a faculty of social welfare,[4] and projects on: technology choice;[5] the changing expectations of society and their relevance for business managers;[6] the links between 'another development' for third world countries and a post-industrial future for the industrialised world;[7] and the process of changing direction which societies and people experience at turning points in their lives.[8] Among published articles and papers, many people have told us that our Turning Point paper on 'The Redistribution of Work'[9] has helped them to clarify their ideas about the future of work. Many discussions on that aspect of the future, as well as meetings and conferences on the future of education, health, social welfare, planning, energy conservation, business management and public policy have helped us to take our own thinking forward. Discussions on these topics with government, business and professional people, students, and a wide variety of lay groups during speaking tours in the United States, Canada and Australia and on shorter visits to many countries in Europe have helped to strengthen our international perspective.

The time has now come for the original text to be substantially revised. Apart from many comparatively minor additions and alterations to bring the references up to date or to clarify the argument at certain points, readers of the earlier edition will find that the following more significant changes have been made.

First, I have followed my American publisher in changing the subtitle of the book from "signposts to a self-fulfilling future' to 'a choice of futures.' Some critics read the original subtitle as suggesting that a benign future could come about with little effort. The new subtitle underlines the need to choose what kind of future we are helping to create, and to act accordingly.

Chapter 3 replaces the former Chapter 2A. In the last five years a welcome shift in mainstream thinking about the future of industrialised economies has begun to take place, and it now seems best to treat the discussion of structural change in the formal economy as part of the main theme of the book.

In Chapter 4 (formerly Chapter 3) part of the section about Work has been rewritten and expanded. This change reflects the welcome growth of public awareness in the past five years that employment may indeed be ceasing to be the universally dominant form of work.

Chapter 6 (formerly Chapter 5) has been expanded too. This may be the most important addition to the earlier text. It aims to explain why the personal, decentralised approach to social transformation — far from being politically naive, as some critics have argued — is more realistic and more likely to succeed than the more conventional reformist and Marxist approaches, both of which are crippled by the self-contradictory realities of power.

Chapter 7 is new. This modest essay in social fiction aims to suggest some aspects of the sane, humane, ecological future for those living in it, and also — by looking back through their eyes — some aspects of the transformation which will bring it about.

My aim in writing this book, and now in revising it, has been to help readers to think about the future — and do something about it — for themselves. So, for those who may find them useful, I have suggested some questions to stimulate discussion and numerous books for further reading. But in this edition I have placed these at the end, in an Appendix and in the References and Bibliography rather than after each chapter. This may be less distracting for readers who wish to read the book straight through, before discussing particular aspects of it or following up references.

Finally, I have omitted the list of people and organisations working for a sane, humane, ecological future, which was included as an Appendix to the first edition. Our contacts of this kind are now so numerous that any such list today would be far too long. The References and Bibliography section contains some relevant entries. The twice-yearly Turning Point[2] newsletters contain many more.

It will be evident that, in my work on the subjects touched on in this book, I have been helped in various ways by many people. Quite a number are mentioned in the text and in the References and Bibliography. But I can think of many others, in a number of countries, to whom I am grateful for the kindness and hospitality, stimulus and encouragement, they have given me in the course of my work. I wish I had enough space to name them all individually.

My principal debt of gratitude, once again, is to my wife, Alison Pritchard. As in the original writing and publication of this book, so in its re-writing and re-publication, she has played an indispensable part.

1
A Choice of Futures

Thinking about the future can be a complicated business. A well-known guidebook to the literature on alternative futures contained reviews of over a thousand items. Reports on alternative futures for the United States have described many possible scenarios, giving them names like 'hitting the jackpot', 'journey to transcendence', 'industrial renaissance', and 'mature calm'. Post-industrial society, super-industrial society, post-civilised society, technetronic society, convivial society, mature society, para-primitive society, psycho-social society, post-scarcity society, a learning and planning society — these are just a few of the ways that individual futurologists have described the particular kind of society they are predicting or recommending for the future. Think-tanks, policy research units, institutes for the future, professional futurists, computer models of the future — all these have proliferated during the last twenty years or so. If we had to discover and understand what they all think about the future, we should never begin to think about it for ourselves.

But we must think about it for ourselves. We can't just leave it to the experts. Experts tend to be narrow and specialised. This means that experts don't see the whole picture, and that different kinds of experts disagree about what is important. Experts make things complicated — either by mistake because they have forgotten how to think simply, or deliberately in order to impress us with their expertise. So-called experts — who, incidentally, are usually men not women — always see the future as a reflection of themselves. If for the black writer James Baldwin 'the future is black', for the nuclear energy expert it is a nuclear energy future, and for the space expert it is a future in which space travel and space colonisation are the key features. In general, if we leave the experts to think about the future for us, we thereby choose a certain kind of future — a future dominated by experts.

So we have to clarify things for ourselves. This means making some fairly simple starting assumptions. Mine are as follows.
(1) There are five distinctly different possibilities for the future, as discussed in this chapter.

10

(2) The next 25 or 30 years will be a critical period in the history of humankind.

(3) Thinking about the future is only useful and interesting if it affects what we do and how we live today.

(4) Practical thinking about the future involves a mixture of the following:

>   predicting what is likely to happen,
>   forecasting what would happen if . . .
>   deciding what we want to happen,
>   planning how to help it to happen;
>   and acting accordingly.

Five Scenarios

Most people incline towards one or another of the following five views (or scenarios) of the future. Each one of the five is assumed by some people to be the only realistic view. How do you feel about each of them? Which one do you prefer? Which do you feel is likely to be closest to the actual future that will happen? I prefer the fifth, and this book is mainly about what it would be like, why it may come about, and how we can help to make it happen. The five views are as follows.

(1) *Business As Usual.* This view holds that the future will be much like the present and the past. There will no doubt continue to be many changes and crises, alarms and excursions, as there always have been. But the main problems of the industrial countries of Europe and North America, and of the world as a whole, will not change dramatically. Nor will the best methods of handling them. Nor will most people's general outlook and attitudes. This view can be presented as the only realistic approach to the practical problems of keeping things going in reasonably good order. It appeals to placid and pragmatic people, good operators, successful trouble-shooters, moderate reformers, people who are content with their present position or their future prospects in the existing system. It also appeals to defeatists, cynics and worldly wisemen, critical of the present state of affairs but convinced they cannot change it and not prepared to try.

(2) *Disaster.* This view holds that things are beginning to break down catastrophically. There is no realistic alternative to nuclear war, and increasing unrest, famine, pollution, poverty, misery, disease and crime on a national and international scale. This view, too, can be presented as the only realistic view of the

11

future. It is held by calm and thoughtful people, who have worked out the possibilities carefully, and who see no point in kidding themselves and others. It also attracts pessimists; hell-fire merchants, preachers and doomsters, who enjoy making other people uncomfortable and who like the limelight themselves; and people whose personal experience of failure has left its mark on their thinking about the world.

(3) *Authoritarian Control (AC).* The right-wing and left-wing variants of this view must be distinguished. The right-wing variant mainly concerns us at this point.

It agrees that the risk of disaster is very real, but holds that the best way to avert it is to accept an authoritarian system of government. People who hold this view point to the emergence of authoritarian regimes at previous crisis periods — Julius Caesar and Augustus after the collapse of the Roman Republic, Napoleon after the French Revolution, Hitler after the Weimar Republic in Germany, Stalin after the Russian Revolution — as evidence that people turn towards authority in times of chaos. They say that worldwide shortages and population pressures are creating a situation in which too many people are competing for too few resources. The only solution to this 'tragedy of the commons' in which uncontrolled individual greed destroys the common good, is as proposed by Hobbes in his 'Leviathan': we must give up our freedom to a sovereign power, which will enforce law and order and distribute the limited resources fairly to us all; otherwise our lives will be poor, solitary, nasty, brutish and short. This view also can be presented persuasively as the only realistic approach to the future. It appeals to people who think they have more to lose from disorder than from dictatorship; to people of an authoritarian, dominating temperament; to people who take a low view of other people ('you can't change human nature'); and to people who think of themselves as belonging to the governing, rather than the governed, class.

The left-wing variant of this view is found among socialists and Marxists. They rely on authoritarian state control as the means of creating a better society. Their approach will be discussed in Chapter 6.

(4) *The Hyper-expansionist (HE) Future.* This view holds that we can break out of our present problems by accelerating the super-industrial drives in Western society, in particular by

making more effective use of science and technology. Space colonisation, nuclear power, computing, and genetic engineering can enable us to overcome the limits of geography, energy, intelligence and biology. This view appeals to optimistic, energetic, ambitious, competitive people for whom economic and technical achievement is more significant than personal and social growth. They are often male. Their preferred future offers bigger toys and more important jobs for the boys. For many of today's opinion-formers, especially in Europe and North America, this is still the only conceivable view of the future — and also an exciting one.

(5) *The Sane, Humane, Ecological (SHE) Future.* This view holds that, instead of accelerating, we should change direction: as I have said elsewhere[11], the key to the future is not continuing expansion but balance — balance within ourselves, balance between ourselves and other people, balance between people and nature. This is not a recipe for no growth. But the crucial new frontiers for growth now are social and psychological, not technical and economic. The only realistic course is to give top priority to learning to live supportively with one another on our small and crowded planet. This will involve decentralisation, not further centralisation. That is the only way of organising that will work. We should aim to create what Willis Harman[12] calls a 'trans-industrial society'. This view appeals to optimistic, participative, reflective people, who reject each of the first four views as unrealistic or unacceptable and believe that a better future is feasible. It has gained increasing acceptance during the last five years[13]. It is only fair to say that it also appeals to quite a large number of cranks.

Of these five views, Business As Usual is the only one which holds, in effect, that we do not need to concern ourselves much with the future; and Disaster is the only one which holds that catastrophe is inevitable. The last three share a serious concern about the future and a common belief that disaster is avoidable. But they disagree with one another about the most effective way of avoiding disaster; and they disagree about what kind of future is most desirable. AC recommends clampdown; HE recommends breakout; and SHE recommends breakthrough. AC and HE are elitist and centralist, while SHE is egalitarian and decentralist. HE and SHE are optimistic, while AC is pessimistic — at least in its right-wing form. AC is restrictive, SHE is conserving, while HE is expansionist.

We need to understand all these different views, because the actual future will almost certainly contain elements of all five: to some extent things will continue as before; to some extent there will be disasters; to some extent the enforcement of new regulations will be needed; to some extent new technologies will help us to break out of existing limits; and to some extent people will develop new ways of living more sanely, more humanely, and more ecologically. Although I prefer the fifth (SHE) view, I certainly don't deny that government and technology both have a positive contribution to make to a sane, humane, ecological world society.

Another reason for trying to understand all five views (and the differences between them) is that the actual future will be shaped by each interacting with the others. The dynamics of this kind of interaction are important. Other people approach the future differently from ourselves; only if we understand how and why, shall we be able to communicate with them, so that they can learn from us and we from them; and, only by succeeding in that, shall we ensure that the actual future turns out well.

So with these points in mind, we now look a little more closely at each of the first four scenarios.

Business As Usual

This scenario is taken for granted by most politicians, business leaders, trade union leaders, media commentators and members of other established institutions today. Whether they take a left-wing or a right-wing view of things generally makes little difference. They have to assume for practical purposes that, although there will continue to be important changes, difficult problems and deep conflicts, no fundamentally new approach or radical rethink is necessary or possible. Their responsibilities in the present, their ambitions for the future and the day-to-day pressures upon them force them to act on business-as-usual assumptions — even if they question these assumptions privately.

In political terms the Business-As-Usual scenario rests on three connected assumptions: that the nation state will remain the prime focus for political action; that representative politicians, political parties, a professional bureaucracy, and institutions representing industry, finance, trade unions and other interest groups, will continue to dominate the processes of politics and government; and that political choices will continue to be made within the broad ideological range of left, right and centre that has come to be taken for granted in the 19th and 20th centuries.

14

In the social sphere, the assumption is that social wellbeing will continue to depend largely on services provided by professional people and organisations — the main point of dispute being the conventional difference of opinion between left and right about whether these services should be paid for directly by their users, or whether they should be financed by taxation or some other form of public funding.

In the economic sphere, it is assumed that the mainspring of economic activity will continue to be manufacturing industry. Wealth will continue to be something which is created by the production and sale of goods, and consumed in the form of goods and services and amenities. The availability of good health, good education, and other forms of social wellbeing, will continue to depend on the prosperity of industries like automobile manufacturing, chemicals, and engineering. The prosperity of the developing countries will continue to depend quite largely on growing markets in the industrial countries. For all these reasons, the top priority will continue to be industrial productivity and economic growth. The main problems, it is assumed, will remain as they are at present. Political debate will continue to centre on how much governments should intervene to secure high levels of industrial investment, high levels of employment and low levels of inflation, and to cushion the social and environmental impacts of industrialisation. There will continue to be a sharp distinction between the economic and social aspects of life, and between work and leisure, work and home. The 'work ethic' will remain strong, in the conventional sense that most men will continue to regard a job as a necessary prerequisite for status and self-esteem, while women identify more with the home and family.

This approach to the future has powerful attractions for many people. First, in terms of power and influence, the people who are well established in the present system of government, economics, social services and professional life, do not want to see it much changed. It is not easy for them to envisage what a different future would be like or how it would work. For example, in spite of growing doubts about the ability of the centralised nation state to handle either international problems or local matters, politicians and government officials find it hard to imagine any practical alternative focus for public affairs. Second, in the sphere of social welfare, people have become accustomed to depend on professional experts and organised services to provide their housing, education, medical treatment, and other forms of care. Many people would find it difficult to envisage an alternative. Third, in the economic sphere, most people (both in industrialised and developing countries) assume that material production, money and jobs are the essential goals of economic activity. The great majority of the world's population still aspire to greater material wellbeing and prosperity. The prospect of material growth has replaced religion as the opium of the people; and the richer and more influential citizens of every country in the world have a vested interest in its continuing credibility, since without it the demand for greater economic equality would be much stronger.

At the same time, the Business-As-Usual approach to the future ignores important questions. How can a world of nation states contain the arms race and the menace of nuclear war? How long can we continue with an asymmetrical economic relationship between the industrial countries and the developing countries of the third world — a relationship in which manufactured goods from the former are exchanged for raw materials and primary commodities from the latter? Are the industrialised countries already hitting physical, psychological, social and organisational limits to further economic growth? These are among the questions which other scenarios try to answer.

Disaster

In the 1970s the Disaster scenario was articulated most clearly by environmentalists. According to Barry Commoner, many people respond to a recitation of the world's environmental problems with deep pessimism. He sees this as the natural aftermath to the shock of recognising that the vaunted 'progress' of modern civilisation is only a thin cloak for global catastrophe.[14] Commoner himself has expressed optimism; he feels that because the environmental crisis arises from our social actions, not from our biological needs, it can be resolved by bringing man's social organisation into harmony with the ecosphere. Paul Ehrlich is more doubtful. Like Barry Commoner, Ehrlich is a biologist. He agrees that, given the necessary changes in human attitude, we could successfully pull through the most dramatic crisis that mankind has faced. But he does not think such a change will occur. As long ago as 1969 Ehrlich said he 'would take even money that England will not exist in the year 2000, and give 10 to 1 that the life of the average Briton would be of distinctly lower quality than it is today.'[14]

The Club of Rome have also been concerned with the prospect of global disaster. Their first report, 'Limits To Growth',[15] had a tremendous impact on many people's thinking about the world's problems. Their second report, 'Mankind At The Turning Point', [16] was published by an international team of scientists and economists in 1975. It said, 'The rapid succession of crises which are currently engulfing the entire globe is the clearest indication that humanity is at a turning point in its historical evolution. The way to make doomsday prophecies self-fulfilling is to ignore the obvious signs of perils that lie ahead. Our scientifically conducted analysis of long term world development based on all available data points out quite clearly that such a passive course leads to disaster.'

Ronald Higgins in 'The Seventh Enemy'[17] described the seven main threats to mankind's survival as:

Population Explosion
Food Shortage
Scarcity of Natural Resources
Pollution and Degradation of the Environment
Nuclear Energy
Uncontrolled Technology
Moral Blindness and Political Inertia.

In Higgins' view, 'We and our children are approaching a world of mounting confusion and horror. The next 25 years, possibly the next decade, will bring starvation to hundreds of millions, and hardship, disorder or war to most of the rest of us. Democracy, where it exists, has little chance of survival, nor in the longer run has our industrial way of life. There will not be a "better tomorrow" beyond our present troubles. That may sound hysterical. Yet it is what the evidence seen as a whole suggests.' Higgins' experience of economics, international diplomacy and central government convinced him that, of his seven threats, the moral blindness of human beings and the painful inertia of our political institutions are what ultimately threaten disaster. The danger is that we will do too little too late to meet the other six threats, because this seventh enemy is too deeply entrenched.

Robert L. Heilbroner[18] shares Ronald Higgins' despair. He concludes that a period of harsh adjustment is coming and he can see no realistic escape: 'If, then, by the question "Is there hope for man?" we ask whether it is possible to meet the challenges of the future without the payment of a fearful price, the answer must be: No, there is no such hope.' John Davoll, an author of 'A Blueprint For Survival'[19] is another whose analysis of the situation leads him towards the pessimism of Higgins and Heilbroner. Davoll is the Director of the Conservation Society in Britain, and in the Society's annual report for 1976[20] he wrote, 'Although environmentalists have realised that a sustainable social and economic system would differ considerably from the existing one, they have usually taken it for granted that the transition from the old order to the new would be reasonably deliberate and orderly; the "Blueprint For Survival" in fact laid down a detailed timetable for the operation. Little attention was given to what political forces might propel this enterprise forward, and it seems to have been tacitly assumed that an intellectual conviction that mankind was heading for trouble, combined with a somewhat blurred vision of a more durable order, would suffice. Recent events have made it clear that anything like this is highly improbable . . . The most probable outcome on the evidence of recent history, is, internally the collapse of democracy into military rule and, externally, general warfare.'

It is difficult to argue convincingly against the likelihood of global disaster, as presented by thinkers like Heilbroner, Higgins and Davoll. The logic of their analysis, powerfully reinforced in the last few years by a spate of books[21] and pamphlets[22] about the dangers and horrors of nuclear war, points so clearly to it. These warnings of disaster are, of course, intended to be constructive. By stressing the gravity of the threat, their authors hope to help us to mobilise the will and strength to achieve the apparently impossible. But we should be careful lest too much dwelling on the prospect of disaster destroy our morale and paralyse our will to act. It is the search for alternatives, for ways of avoiding disaster, that should occupy our minds — not the prophecies of doom.

The next three scenarios offer three possibilities for avoiding disaster and creating a sustainable future. They are based on the authoritarian control (AC) approach, the hyper-expansionist (HE) approach, and the sane, humane, ecological (SHE) approach. Respectively they prescribe, as I have said, clampdown, breakout, and breakthrough.

Authoritarian Control

'People must be restrained, and the only question is how to go about achieving the necessary ends with the least odious and most effective means. . . The rationale for world government with major coercive powers is overwhelming, raising the most fundamental of all political questions: Who should rule, and how?' So writes William Ophuls in 'Leviathan Or Oblivion'.[23] Although Ophuls mentions Aldous Huxley's 'Brave New World' as one possibility, he himself favours a return to the face-to-face life of small communities as a constituent part of planetary government. However, he says, 'only a sovereign would be strong enough to exact the sacrifices needed to return to the simple life.' Ophuls does not welcome the prospect of authoritarian government. He explicitly expresses antipathy to it. But he is among an increasing number of thinkers about the future of politics and government who fear there may be no alternative.

In considering the prospect of a future in which control by authoritarian government would play a central part, we have to consider who wants it, how likely it is, and whether it would work if it came about.

Very few people admit that they would welcome this kind of future. But there are quite a lot who undoubtedly would. Superior, censorious, insecure people like to see other people kept in their place. Among the professional, business, financial and bureaucratic middle classes in the countries of North America and Western and Eastern Europe today there are many who fear the prospect of disorder more than they fear the prospect of neo-fascism or neo-stalinism. In times of uncertainty there will always be many members of the police and military forces ready to impose law and order with a firm hand. So, although I don't want an AC future myself (which is one reason why I think it so important to work for a viable future of a different kind), I realise that there are many people who would welcome it.

A realistic view must put the likelihood of an AC future quite high — as thinkers like Ophuls do. Centralised authoritarian control could fairly easily encroach as a natural and painless, indeed necessary, development from the rather muddled kind of corporate state that has been evolving in countries like Britain since the second world war, and from the expanding role of government in countries like the United States. There are, as I have said, many people who would welcome it, and many others who would be prepared to accept it as the only practical alternative to disaster if law and order began to collapse. If we are to avoid an AC future, we have to recognise that its probability is quite high, and we have to understand the viewpoint of people who would welcome it or accept it.

The third question is crucially important: would an AC future actually work? It is often taken for granted that authoritarian government would be effective, although perhaps undesirable. This seems to be assumed especially by North American thinkers who have never experienced how muddled and inefficient centralised bureaucratic government actually is. I won't repeat what I said about this in 'Power, Money and Sex'.[11] But the evidence suggests that, the more totalitarian they are, the more the 'proliferative and self-serving character of almost all known bureaucracies' (John Davoll) is

19

compounded with incompetence. There is virtually no hard evidence — only wishful thinking — to suggest that authoritarian government (or more regulations than we have in countries like Britain today) would provide effective means to surmount the crises of the next twenty five or thirty years.

Thus the AC scenario is unacceptable on two counts: it would be nasty; and it wouldn't work.

The two remaining alternatives — the HE future and the SHE future — are based on the view that, instead of clamping down, we should seek to break out or break through. They both stand towards the AC philosophy much as the free market philosophy of Adam Smith stood towards the authoritarian restrictionist philosophy of Hobbes. They are both concerned not so much with the protection and allocation of the limited space and resources already available, as with the creation of new space and new resources — physical and economic in the one case, psychological and social in the other. Both are more positive and optimistic than the AC approach. But the directions which they envisage for the future are diametrically opposed.

Hyper-Expansion (HE)

Exponents of this view include Herman Kahn[24] and Daniel Bell.[25] It holds that the human race, having expanded over every part of planet Earth since the 15th century, is now poised to colonise space; that scientific knowledge, having advanced ever more rapidly since the 16th and 17th centuries, is now about to capture the commanding heights of biology, psychology, communication and control; and that industrialism, having developed a dominating economic role since the 18th and 19th centuries, is now bringing super-industrial society to birth. A splendid future now beckons Western, scientific, industrial man if only he has the courage of his convictions.

Kahn believes that we are now at the mid-point of a 400-year period that began 200 years ago with the industrial revolution. 'We have just seen in the most advanced countries the initial emergence of super-industrial economies (where enterprises are extraordinarily large, encompassing and pervasive forces in both the physical and societal environments), to be followed soon by post-industrial economies (where the task of producing the necessities of life has become trivially easy because of technological advancement and economic development). We expect that almost all countries eventually will develop the characteristics of super- and post-industrial

20

societies'. Writing in 1977, Kahn believed that 'barring extreme mismanagement or bad luck, the period 1976-1985 should be characterised by the highest average rate of world economic growth in history.' In general, he presents what he calls 'a plausible scenario for a "growth" world that leads not to disaster but to prosperity and plenty.'

Bell specifies the following five components of what he calls post-industrial society:
(1)   Economic sector: the change from a goods-producing to a service economy;
(2)   Occupational distribution: the pre-eminence of the professional and technical class;
(3)   Axial principle: the centrality of theoretical knowledge as the source of innovation and of policy formulation for the society;
(4)   Future orientation: the control of technology and technology assessment;
(5)   Decision making: the creation of a new intellectual technology.

The Hyper-Expansionist or super-industrial future is thus seen as a logical extension of the industrial past. Just as the economies of today's industrial countries progressed historically from the primary commodity stage to the secondary manufacturing stage, so now they are progressing through the tertiary service stage towards the quaternary service-to-service stage. Among the growing points in an economy of this kind are universities, research institutes and consultancies, and industries like aerospace, telecommunications and computing. All these provide services to sectors like transport, communications and finance, which themselves provide services to corporations and individuals. Shifting the emphasis into these knowledge-based, high technology industries and services will, according to this scenario, enable today's industrial countries to retain their markets in the developing countries as the latter enter fully on the industrial manufacturing stage.

The Hyper-Expansionist scenario shares the underlying assumptions of the Business-As-Usual scenario, that 'wealth' is created by the provision and sale of goods and services which other people and other countries will be willing to buy, and that expansion can continue indefinitely. The prospect of space colonisation is an important element in it. So is the further development of nuclear power as an energy source. The Hyper-Expansionist scenario shares the Business-As-Usual scenario's assumption that the economic relationship between the industrialised and developing countries will continue to be asymmetrical, with the former continuing to lead the latter along the path of economic progress. But the Hyper-Expansionist scenario is more challenging than the Business-As-Usual scenario. It holds that the future for today's industrialised countries lies in accelerating the shift from conventional manufacturing industry to the high technology, know-how, and professional service industries; and that the underlying task for the business system (and for public policy) in those countries is to manage this transition successfully.

This scenario conforms to the widespread assumption that progress means increasing technical sophistication and the extrapolation of existing trends. But it also raises many unsolved questions — technical, political, and psychological. The feasibility of widespread automation, space colonisation, and massive nuclear power programmes in the next few decades is not assured. When the basic needs of billions of third world people are not yet met, will it be possible for the industrialised countries to concentrate on creating a high technology future? In the industrialised countries themselves transitional unemployment would be very high. Society would be polarised between a comparatively small number of experts and technocrats on the one hand and the leisured irresponsible masses on the other. Even if it did prove possible to make the transition to that kind of society, would it satisfy the higher level needs of most people for self-esteem and self-fulfilment? It is not at all clear how the hyper-expansionist approach would break out of the limits which (as we shall see) seem now to be closing in on the developed economies of today.

Sane, Humane, Ecological (SHE)

Five years ago it was still widely assumed that the HE future was the only possible post-industrial future. But, as Michael Marien was one of the first to show, there have for many years been two conflicting meanings of 'post-industrial' and two completely different visions of post-industrial society. Marien[26] described the first as the vision of a technological, affluent, service society, and the second as the vision of a decentralised agrarian economy following in the wake of the failure of industrialism. (As thus described, the second gave rather too negative an impression of what I call the SHE view of the future.) In the last five years, the two opposing visions, HE and SHE, of post-industrial society have become much more widely understood. Their opposition now provides the focus for much informed discussion of the future.

22

The SHE view perceives the present crisis of industrial society and the world as a crisis of masculine values. It regards the HE view as a dangerous masculine fantasy — exploitative, elitist and unsympathetic. It believes that the line of social progress shaped by the technical and economic imperatives of the industrial age has reached its limit. The breakthrough now needed is on a different front. It will focus on the needs and capacities of people.

A Historical Perspective

Later chapters will discuss different aspects of the SHE future and how it can be achieved. The rest of this chapter discusses what insights about it can be gained by looking back into the past.

The fall of the Roman Empire is often quoted as a turning point in history that is comparable to the present time. Heilbroner[27] is one of those who holds the view that humankind is now entering a new dark age. He pessimistically likens our present prospects to the Roman Empire's period of decline in the 5th and 6th centuries AD, when 'the established institutions of the Empire gradually lost their ability to cope with the orderly provision of the former Roman territories, and in which a deep and pervasive crisis of faith simultaneously destroyed the Empire from within.' William Irwin Thompson[28] makes the same comparison between that period and this, but he sees the dark ages as creative periods. He instances the 6th century Christian monastery school of Lindisfarne (on Holy Island, Northumberland, England) as an example of a small, short-lived community creating new light and vitalising old philosophies against a background of darkness and destruction. In establishing a contemporary Lindisfarne Institute, Thompson and his colleagues tried to go 'back on the spiral to the pre-industrial community to create, on a higher plane with the most advanced scientific and spiritual thought we can achieve, the planetary, meta-industrial village ... We are trying to create an educational community that can become a mutational deme in which cultural evolution can move from civilisation to planetisation.' L. S. Stavrianos, in 'The Promise Of The Coming Dark Age.'[29] also looks on the Dark Age following the collapse of Rome as an age of epochal creativity, when values and institutions were evolved that constitute the bedrock foundation of modern civilisation. The Dark Age was an age of birth as well as of death; a dynamic and seminal phase in human history. Stavrianos shows that the present shares four important features with that period — economic imperialism, ecological degradation, bureaucratic ossification and a flight from reason. But these parallels between the two periods lead Stavrianos to an optimistic and constructive view of the future. He sees it in terms of a movement from aristo-technology to demo-technology, from boss control to worker control, from representative democracy to participatory democracy, and from self-subordination to self-actualisation.

Thus, looking back to the fall of the Roman Empire may throw some light on the possibilities for our future today.

But there is a more telling approach. If we do indeed stand at the beginning of a new future, then we must also be standing at the end of an old past. What is this past that we are leaving? The more clearly we identify it and the better we understand its nature, the more clearly we shall understand the future upon which we are now entering.

Are we, then, coming to the end of a 200 year period in history — the period which was shaped by the emergence of representative political democracy in the American and French revolutions and by the industrial revolution? Does this mean we should look forward to post-representative politics and a post-industrial revolution? Murray Bookchin[30] is among those who look back 200 years for a period comparable to the present time. He finds it in the revolutionary Enlightenment that swept through France in the 18th century — a period which, as he says, completely reworked French consciousness and prepared the conditions for the Great Revolution of 1789. A distintegrating social process was taking place in which the ancient regime lost credibility, in which a vast critique of the old system developed, and in which more and more people began spontaneously to withdraw their support from it. Bookchin feels that the same thing is happening today, but it is a century and a half of embourgeoisement that is now breaking down and bourgeois institutions that are collapsing. There is, indeed, much attraction in the idea of a post-industrial revolution which would be today's counterpart to the industrial revolution. It would bring a new breakthrough in psychological and social development comparable in importance with the economic and technical breakthrough of 200 years ago. In Chapter 5 I shall suggest some parallels between how the industrial revolution happened and the kind of process the post-industrial revolution could be.

But perhaps we should be looking back not 200 years but 500. Are we now coming to the end of the individualist, scientific, European period of world history which began with the Renaissance and the Reformation? Should we be looking forward now to a less

24

individualistic, post-scientific, post-European era?

Three changes which mark the transition from the Middle Ages to modern times seem to have particular relevance for us today. The first was the shift from the religious outlook of the Middle Ages to the political and economic values of the post-Reformation age. The second was the growing need people felt in the 15th and 16th centuries to liberate themselves from the domination of mediaeval institutions, especially the Church, which prevented a sense of personal contact with reality. The third was the growing artificiality and incredibility of the traditional intellectual framework — the theological structure elaborated by the schoolmen — which ultimately led to its collapse. All of these have important parallels today.

R.H. Tawney in 'Religion And The Rise Of Capitalism'[31] described how the theological mould which shaped political theory in the Middle Ages was broken at the Renaissance. Machiavelli emancipated the state from religion; politics became a science; reason took the place of revelation; and the basis for political institutions became expedience, not religious authority. Somewhat later an objective and passionless economic science also emerged. Thus politics and economics became self-contained departments of life in their own right, and religion was relegated to a self-contained department of its own. More recently, Gurth Higgin[32] has also described how the 'social project' of mediaeval society was religion. Beliefs about reality, sanctions for social order, and the reasons behind all activities, were directly derived from religion. Adherence to them was seen as serving religion. This did not mean that everyone was religious all the time. But it did mean that most people were concerned with their religious condition; that, as the mediaeval cathedrals testify, the Church was the dominant institution of society; and that theology was the queen of the sciences. Then 'the settled religious social project of the Middle Ages began to lose its power, and — in spite of a bitter and vigorous rearguard action — its leading part, the Church, also finally suffered decline. Western European societies were developing a new social project, a social project that replaced religion by economic values. . . . Whereas in the Middle Ages the most heinous crimes were blasphemy, heresy, witchcraft and other crimes against religion, in the new order the most serious crimes are those against property and in particular its symbol, money.'

Higgin goes on to compare that transition from the Middle Ages to modern times with the transition we are entering upon today. He suggests that it is now the turn of the economic 'social project' to wither, and along with it its 'leading social part' (manufacturing industry) and its 'leading psychological part' (alienating willingness to dedicate one's life to being merely an instrument of work). 'The name of the game in the Middle Ages was religion. The name of the game in the industrial era is economics. What it might be in the more distant future nobody knows.'

My guess is that the new name of the game will be to do with human growth, in a social, ecological and spiritual perspective; and that religion, politics and economics will come together again in this new vision of the meaning of life.

The Renaissance and the Reformation brought about personal liberation and the collapse of the old conceptual framework by stressing the value of direct experience and observation at the expense of received doctrine and authority. The religious symbolism of mediaeval art gave way to human realism, and eventually artists like Leonardo relied almost entirely on study and experiment as the best guide to the truth, not on tradition and convention. Luther argued that Christians needed no elaborate paraphernalia of religious ceremonies and ecclesiastical institutions to teach them their duty or to correct them if they neglected it: let them listen to the scriptures and their own conscience. Luther felt that to externalise religion in rules and ordinances was to degrade it. The Bible should be translated out of Latin into languages that people could understand.

Today a similarly compelling desire to make closer personal contact with reality is widely felt. It shows itself as a growing interest in decentralised energy systems — solar panels, windmills, etc. — which put individuals and households more directly in touch with natural energy sources; as a desire to grow more more of our own food and to do more things for ourselves, and thus to be more directly in touch with the materials and natural resources on which we depend; and as an urge to develop our own capacities for spiritual experience and explore our own consciousness, rather than being content with the ceremonies and doctrines of formal religion as mediated to us by priests. In general it shows itself in a growing desire to liberate ourselves from the institutional and intellectual structures of modern society which have become buffers between ourselves and what we feel is real.

Meanwhile, the highly specialised mumbo-jumbo of economists and social scientists seems less and less relevant to real needs. 'New generations of researchers are inculcated with an orthodox vision elaborated with more and more concrete details. The increasing amount of empirical findings accumulated and organised within the given conceptual framework requires an increased effort on the part of the individual who would learn the state of the field. It also creates more questions than it settles and tends, therefore, to lead to increasing specialisation. When this happens it becomes more and more difficult for the individual to avoid scientific myopia, and to keep his subject in perspective and maintain a dispassionate overview of the entire field. In particular, it becomes difficult to keep in mind that alternative, latent visions, capable of organising the same collections of "facts," must always exist — or to imagine what these alternatives would be'.[33] Are economists and social scientists now performing the role which the schoolmen performed in the dying Middle Ages? Are the economic and social sciences losing credibility as a guide to action, just as theology lost credibility in the 15th and 16th centuries?[34]

But perhaps 500 years is not enough. Perhaps, in order to understand what age is now ending for us, we should look back 2000 years to the beginning of the era which took its character from the Hebrew, Greek and Roman civilisations. Astrologers call it the Age of Pisces and say that the Age of Aquarius is now beginning. Most of us think of it as the Christian era. Will the future age be the age of a post-Christian planetary culture?

There are certainly some interesting parallels between the situation now and that which existed 2000 years ago. For example, Jewish religious law had become formalised and fossilised, like our overdeveloped institutions today. It was 'forgotten that the Law was designed as an aid to rectitude, not as an end in itself. Correct observance was so manifold and took up so much time that the majority of simpler souls had pardonably arrived at the tacit conclusion that such outward obedience was all that mattered. Prayer, probity, charity, and moral soundness in general had become regarded as a species of tax payable to the deity, rather than a means of communion with the deity. The ideal, organic relationship between man and god was threatening to turn into just such a fortuitous and inconsequential one as characterised the pagan creeds. Abstract monotheism too had become very much externalised. This state of affairs was what Jesus set out to remedy'.[35]

Second, just as Roman imperialism and administration had then created conditions for the mediterranean world in which Christianity could spread and flourish, so today European imperialism and modern technologies of transport and communication have created conditions favourable to the spread of a single planetary culture. As Jesus, John

27

and Paul then brought together the spiritual, intellectual and organising genius of the Hebrew, Greek and Roman traditions to create the foundations for a new world religion and civilisation, so today various strands seem to be converging — for example, from sub-atomic physics, from ecology, from systems theory, from Eastern mysticism, from humanistic psychology and from the Christianity of Teilhard de Chardin — to create a new planetary movement from which a new civilisation may spring.[36] As the early spread of Christianity took off, so perhaps we should now be prepared for a new world movement to blossom and spread. In the early Christian movement martyrdom was of the essence, following the example of Christ; and part of the combat training of the early Christians was to discuss the sufferings and deaths of their martyred friends in order to prepare themselves to endure similar torture and humiliation when their time came. Will non-violence be the central principle of action in the new planetary movement that is in prospect now? Will an important feature of the new movement be the sharing of experience of non-violent action, and the training of one another for it?

So, industrial revolution, Renaissance and Reformation, the beginning of the Christian era — which of these should we regard as the beginning of the age which is now ending? From which can we learn the most relevant insights about the future which we face today? The answer is all three.

First, by contrast with the main characteristics of the last 200, 500 and 2000 years, we can identify important characteristics of the future which we now face. In place of the technical progress and economic expansion that has characterised the industrial age, we shall emphasise human development and quality of life. In place of the European values and analytical type of knowledge that have dominated the world in the post-Renaissance age, a planetary civilisation will emerge in which intuitive understanding plays a larger role. In place of the masculine, unecological values that have underpinned Christendom for the last 2000 years, based on the idea of God, the Father, giving Man dominion over the earth, we shall shift to more feminine, more ecological modes of perceiving, doing and being.

Second, by comparison with what happened at those historical watersheds, we can see what kind of process of change we face today. The old structure has become institutionalised and sterile; conditions have been created in which a new movement, capturing new energies, can spread and flourish; the new movement will be based on the urge to break through to more direct contact and communion with reality; the new movement will become self-sustaining in ways that owe comparatively little to the dominant mechanisms and motivating drives of the age that is passing. These features of the historical watersheds of 200, 500, and 2000 years ago are features of our situation today.

Thus each of these three periods of history and the way they began can give us useful insights. They tell us something about the nature of the post-industrial, post-European, post-Christian future — the sane, humane, ecological future — which is now beginning; and they give us some ideas about the nature of the transition to it.

2
A New Economic Direction

Conventional economic expansion is hitting limits.

In the 1970s the emphasis was on physical limits. The energy crisis, pollution of the environment, and the threat of world population outrunning the planet's resources, caused many people to question the possibility of continuing economic growth on conventional lines.

In the 1980s the emphasis has shifted. Higher levels of unemployment in many countries have caused people to ask whether full employment can ever be restored as a permanent feature of economic life. Is there a limit to the amount of work in society that can be organised by employers through the labour market? Is this limit now closing in? Does this mean that more people should be enabled to organise work for themselves?

The present crisis of work does not mean that awareness of the energy and resources problem has faded from the public mind. That awareness remains, and many people are now actively concerned to create a more conserving society. It is just that the main focus for public debate has, for the time being, shifted to the crisis of work. In the later 1980s new issues will no doubt invade the public mind. Health and welfare — what are they? and how are people to achieve them? — could be one. By reaching crisis proportions in its turn, that issue — and then others — will reinforce the doubts about a business-as-usual economy which the energy crisis of the 'seventies and the work crisis of the early 'eighties have already planted in people's minds.

In this chapter I shall summarise the limits now closing in on the business-as-usual economy, and outline some of the main economic features of the path that will lead towards a SHE future.

Limits to Conventional Economic Expansion
(1) Physical Limits

The fixed dimensions and finite resources of planet Earth cannot allow conventional economic growth to continue indefinitely. This general hypothesis has been increasingly accepted as common sense since the publication of 'Limits To Growth'[15] in 1972, in spite of economists' counter attacks and technical criticisms from other academics and scientists. As Emile Benoit has pointed out, the thinking of classical economists such as J. S. Mill about a 'stationary state' of economic activity has now been integrated with the insights of ecology and the imagery of the space age — for example by Kenneth Boulding in 'The Economics Of The Coming Spaceship Earth'.[23] Benoit[37] summarises the new situation as follows: 'Our earth, we now begin to realise, does not and cannot supply us with an unlimited amount of usable energy, raw materials, foodstuffs, safe dumping grounds for our waste products — or even standing room. It is not an inexhaustible cornucopia. It is much more like an inter-planetary vehicle, where resources must be carefully conserved, waste products must be minimised and recycled, and where the number of passengers must be carefully limited to those that can be taken aboard without overcrowding... We have, in effect, a revolution of rising expectation, superimposed on a population explosion, in a world of fixed dimensions and limited productive capacity. Therein lies the problem.'

Complicated, and sometimes heated, technical arguments will no doubt continue to be exchanged among experts about how soon the planet's resources may run out and how soon this strictly physical limit may be reached. Similarly, technical arguments will continue to be heard about the scope for improving the efficiency with which energy and resources are used. Such debate can throw light on specific points concerning the use of resources. But it does not affect the main issue. Mounting pressure on the carrying capacity of the earth, combined with increasing resistance to the present inequitable distribution of the earth's resources among its peoples, must soon begin to push us towards permanently sustainable patterns of economic activity. Common sense suggests that we should be moving towards them as quickly as we can. We probably have no more than twenty-five or thirty years to achieve them, if catastrophic disasters affecting most of humankind and the planet are to be avoided.

(2) *Social Limits*

As Fred Hirsch pointed out in 'Social Limits To Growth',[38] the expansion of the formal economy tends to decrease the value of socially scarce goods once they are attained. He cited traffic congestion and higher education as examples. The satisfaction derived from an automobile depends on the traffic conditions in which it can be used, and these will deteriorate as use becomes more widespread. The competitive value of higher education as a launching pad for a good job, goes down as the number of highly educated people goes up; as access to higher education spreads, its 'positional' value declines. Hirsch contrasted the positional economy with what he called the material economy in which what one person enjoys does not reduce the value of what other people enjoy. He defined the positional economy as covering everything that is either scarce in itself or subject to congestion by extensive use; and he pointed out that, 'as general standards of living rise... competition moves increasingly from the material sector to the positional sector, where what one wins another loses in a zero-sum game. As the frontier closes, positional competition intensifies... In the positional sector, individuals chase each other's tails. The race gets longer for the same prize.'

In other words, many of the goods delivered by the formal economy become progressively less valuable as it grows. Eventually a limit is reached. The advanced industrial countries are not far off it now, in many respects.

(3) *Institutional Limits*

As the formal economy has developed, it has become increasingly complex, institutionalised and congested. It has now reached the point where the supposedly wealth-creating activities of industry and commerce are generating such great social costs, and the interrelations between industry, finance, government, trade unions, and the public services have become so intertwined, that the workings of the system are grinding towards a halt. The American counter-economist, Hazel Henderson, describes this as 'the entropy state' which, she says, 'is a society at the stage when complexity and interdependence have reached such unmodelable, unmanageable proportions that its transaction costs equal or exceed its productive capabilities. In a manner analogous to physical systems, the society winds down of its own weight and the proportion of its gross national product that must be spent in mediating conflicts, controlling crime, footing the bill for all the social costs generated by the externalities of production and consumption, providing ever more comprehensive bureaucratic co-ordination, and generally trying to maintain "social homeostasis", begins to grow exponentially or even hyper-exponentially. Such societies may have already drifted to a soft-landing in a steady state, with inflation masking their declining condition'.[39]

(4) *Psychological Limits*

As more and more people in industrialised societies have come to depend for more and more aspects of our lives on remote, impersonal institutions rather than directly on our own efforts and those of people we know and live with at home and in our local community, our sense of personal responsibility has been eroded and our sense of alienation has deepened. Many specific examples could be given of the kind of behaviour that results. On the right these would include speculation, profiteering, asset-stripping and other accepted but exploitative forms of organised money-grubbing. On the left they would include strikes and industrial action by public service workers in health, education and transport. In general, what results is that we all tend to make greater claims on the economy — for money, for jobs, for goods and commercial services, and for public and social services — while, at the same time becoming less willing to contribute whole-heartedly to it. In other words, because we do not experience economic activity in terms of personal involvement with other people, we try to get more out of the economy than we put in. We try to get something for nothing, from society as well as from the natural environment in which we live.

It is obvious what must happen. Sooner or later the time comes when our demands outrun the economy's capacity to meet them. At this point the money-based economy becomes locked into a combination of rising inflation, unemployment, public expenditure and taxes. All of these are experienced as intolerably high, but attempts to reduce any of them make some of the others worse and inflict hardship on many people. From now on, conventional economic policies of any kind — right, left or centre — only compound the problem. The economic consequences of the political shifts that have taken place, whether from left to right or from right to left, in Britain, France, the United States, and even in Sweden and West Germany in the last few years, have demonstrated this quite clearly.

(5) *Conceptual Limits*

As the physical limits and the social, institutional and psychological limits to conventional economic growth have become more and more apparent in the last ten to fifteen years, conventional economic thinking — which assumes that those limits do not exist — has begun to lose credibility. As more and more people realise that there are limits to what we can expect from the planet and what we can expect from other people, the previously accepted intellectual framework for understanding how the economy works — the prevailing paradigm of economic life — is beginning to crumble.

For example, the idea that wealth is created by extracting the resources of the earth, turning them into manufactured products, selling them to people, who use them and throw them away as waste

33

— and that the faster this process can be repeated the more wealth is created — seems more questionable now that it did twenty years ago. Again, the notion that wealth is something that must be created by industry and commerce before it can be spent on the provision of social wellbeing by public services is wearing thin. Increasingly, people are asking why it should be necessary to build and sell more automobiles in order to be able to afford more schools and teachers; or why it should be necessary to make and sell more cigarettes and sweets in order to be able to afford more doctors and dentists. They are asking: what sort of 'wealth' is this, which is created and consumed in this way? and they are increasingly coming up with answers like the following: 'To the indiscriminate growth economists it doesn't matter whether the products of industrial activity are more sweets to rot the children's teeth, or insulating blocks for houses. Essentially, the concern is with measured economic busyness rather than with purposes.'[40]

The idea that wealth, or national product, is created only by activity in the money-based, institutional sector of the economy and not by activity in the informal domestic and local community sector — for example, that the economic production of the country actually goes down if people grow their own vegetables instead of buying them in the shops — is also wearing thin. As Hugh Stretton has put it in 'Housing and Government', 'How easily we could turn the tables on the economists if we all decided that from tomorrow morning, the work of the domestic economy should be paid for. Instead of cooking dinner for her own lot, each housewife would feed her neighbours at regular rates; then they'd cook for her family and get their money back. We'd do each other's housework and gardening at award rates. Big money would change hands when we fixed each other's tap washers and electric plugs at the plumbers' and electricians' rates. Without a scrap of extra work Gross National Product (GNP) would go up by a third overnight. We would increase that to half if the children rented each other's back yards and paid each other as play supervisors, and we could double it if we all went to bed next door at regular massage parlor rates. Our economists would immediately be eager to find out what line of investment was showing such fabulous growth in capital/output ratio. They'd find that housing was bettered only by double beds and they'd recommend a massive switch of investment into both. Don't laugh, because in reverse, this nonsense measures exactly the distortion we get in our national accounts now'.[41]

Economists are, in fact, increasingly beginning to claim that GNP has never purported to measure the 'use value' of economic activity; they have always recognised that it simply represents the 'exchange value' of all goods and services produced in the money economy; it does not differentiate between desirable and undesirable economic activity; nor does it differentiate between final economic consumption and intermediate economic activity which is undertaken to treat disease, clean up pollution, salvage accidents and mitigate damage caused by other economic activities. Some analysts are actually suggesting that rising GNP in industrialised countries now measures mainly the rising costs of pollution, environmental degradation and human suffering; and although that cannot be proved, it is a further indication of the declining credibility of rising GNP either as a measure of economic wellbeing or as a desirable goal of economic endeavour.

In fact, conventional economics is blind to so much of obvious importance that it is coming to be seen, following Hazel Henderson's suggestion[39], as a form of brain damage. Can it broaden into a new discipline based on more realistic theories and techniques of personal and social choice? Or will it, as happened in the past to alchemy, find itself stranded on the shores of history as the tide goes out? Have economists still got a useful contribution to make to our choices for the future and how to bring them about? Is it still worthwhile trying to speak to economists, and to think in their language and categories of thought, about questions of genuine concern? Twenty years ago these questions hardly arose. Soon, as the limits to the credibility of economics continue to become more apparent, they will be commonplace.

A SHE Economic Path

There is thus a whole variety of ways in which the thrust of conventional economic activity is bumping against limits. This applies to the world economy as a whole, but in particular to the industrialised countries. Different people emphasise the importance of different limits. But in general it is becoming clear that a change of direction will have to take place. We can follow no further the path of development we have been on for the last two or three hundred years. We must now set out on a new one.

What will this path be like, and how shall we recognise it? Those are the questions we need to ask. We don't need to draw up a blueprint for a static society at some date in the future. The society of

35

the future probably won't be static. In any case, the practical questions for us are what shall we do now? What path shall we take now?

A SHE economic path will shift the priorities to human needs, social justice and ecological sustainability. It will not aim for no growth, but for healthy growth instead of cancerous growth. It will aim for equilibrium or steady state economics, in the sense of preferring activities that can be sustainable — what Schumacher called the economics of permanence.[42]

In this section I shall try to convey a sense of the changes that will be required in the world economy today, and in particular in the industrialised countries, if we are to move along this path. I hope this will help to clarify some of the practical consequences of these impending changes — not only as they will affect us as men and women with our personal lives to live, but also as they will affect us in our more specialised roles as business people, doctors, planners, politicians, government officials, trade unionists, bankers, public servants, teachers, and so on. But, first, two general points.

A SHE economy will not involve returning to pre-industrial conditions, with poverty and subsistence farming as the prevailing mode of life. This is sometimes alleged by people who cannot conceive an acceptable alternative to perpetual economic expansion. The truth is that by moving along a SHE economic path, based on sane, humane, ecological use of advanced technology, mankind will have a better chance of meeting economic needs and achieving a high quality of life, than by trying to prolong the conventional trajectory of economic growth beyond its feasible limits.

The second point is this. Many conservationists stress the physical limits to further economic expansion, but are less aware of the social, psychological, institutional and conceptual limits. They tend to assume that authoritarian controls will be needed — and will be able — to impose economic equilibrium. In Chapter 1, in the context of the AC scenario, we saw reason to doubt the capability of authoritarian governments to do this successfully. Here we question the need. As the limits to conventional economic growth continue to press more heavily, more and more people whose basic material needs are secure will turn their attention elsewhere. They will relax, not intensify, competition with one another for formal economic success. Some will turn to household and neighbourhood production of goods and services previously provided by big corporations or the state. For others, psychological and social growth will take priority over the

36

economic, materialist rat-race. There is plenty of evidence that this is happening already. One example is the 'voluntary simplicity'[43] movement in North America. In Britain, one recent survey[44] reported that the British have become 'remarkably unambitious in a material sense. Very few sincerely want to be rich. Most people in Britain neither want nor expect a great deal more money. Even if they could get it, the vast majority do not seem prepared to work harder for it: most respondents thought they should only work as much as they needed to live a pleasant life. What's more the British seem to have lowered their sights since 1973 ... There appears to be a new phenomenon: a revolution of falling expectations.'

The following will be among the most important features of a SHE economic path.

(1) *Energy and Resources*

A SHE economy will reflect the principles of ecology. The way people use resources will reflect the way resources are used in nature. The economic system will become an integral part of the larger ecological system, i.e. a closed loop of material cycles powered by the sun.

In making the transition to an equilibrium economy we will, as Kenneth Boulding[23] says, be leaving the open 'cowboy' economy of the past in which humankind was able to exploit the apparently limitless spaces and resources of an under-populated planet, and entering a closed economy in which the earth has become a single spaceship without unlimited reservoirs of anything either for extraction or for pollution, and in which therefore people must find their place in a cyclical ecological system.

Like any well-managed enterprise, this kind of permanently sustainable equilibrium economy will use income, not capital, to meet its recurrent needs. It will depend on renewable energy supplies from sun or wind or water or natural vegetation, and not on exhaustible once-for-all deposits of fossil fuels. Manufacturing industry will process and reprocess renewable and recyclable materials, rather than convert unrenewable and exhaustible materials into products which are later thrown away as waste. Agricultural production similarly will become a self-sustaining process in which renewable sources of fertility will be used as a perpetual source of income, rather than a once-for-all process of using up physical capital (in the form of natural soil fertility, and of chemical fertilisers and pesticides derived from fossil fuels and other exhaustible mineral deposits).[45]

(2) *Lower Throughput, Greater Durability*

Compared with today's pattern of economic activity in the industrial countries, a SHE economy will place greater emphasis on the durability of manufactured products. Repair and maintenance and servicing will become relatively more important than they are today. What people need in order to enjoy a high quality of life will be more clearly distinguished from what they can be persuaded to want by advertising and promotional techniques.[46]

(3) *People First, Things Second*

The industrial economy of the last 200 years has focussed primarily on things and organisations. As consumers, people have become accustomed to want more things, and as workers they have become accustomed to subordinate themselves to the requirements of factories, machines, and assembly lines. In a SHE economy the production and distribution of things will become a relatively less important part of the economy than the provision of services, care and amenity for people; the processes of producing and distributing things will be carried out as if people matter; and services, care and amenity will increasingly be provided by people for themselves and one another.

A SHE economy will rely more heavily on the energies and skills of people than the industrial or hyper-expansionist economies. This will not mean going back to the bad old days of labour-intensive drudgery. It means that people's energies and skills will be recognised as an important renewable resource, as contrasted with the unrenewable energy and materials required to make and operate capital-intensive plant; and it means that satisfying and rewarding occupation will be an important economic objective in itself. In the industrial economy the employment of people has represented a cost which employers aimed to reduce. In a SHE economy, it is the reduction of opportunities for personally satisfying and socially useful occupation that will be regarded as a cost; high priority will be given to developing the activities, the technologies and the kind of organisations required to make such opportunities widely available. In terms of Abraham Maslow's[47] hierarchy of needs, the industrial economy has concentrated on meeting people's physiological needs and need for safety, whereas the emphasis in a SHE economy will shift towards also meeting people's higher level needs for belongingness and love, esteem, and self-actualisation.[48]

(4) *Self-Reliance and Mutual Aid*

Ever since Adam Smith began the 'Wealth of Nations' by describing the advantages of specialisation in the manufacturing of pins, the industrial economy has been based on the idea that progress involves greater and greater economic specialisation, differentiation and interdependence. The Hyper-Expansionist view of the future not only accepts this idea, but argues for accelerated progress of this kind, for example in areas like knowledge, leisure and personal care. A SHE economy, while recognising that some degree of specialisation is valuable, will also recognise that there are desirable limits to it and that in many respects those limits have been exceeded. In practice, therefore, a SHE economic path will put more emphasis on self-reliance than on further specialisation.

As a general rule, each country, each region, each district, each locality and each household will aim to be rather more self-sufficient economically, and rather less dependent on uncontrollable outside sources of goods and services, than is the case in the world economy and in national and local economies today. For example, there will be a prevailing tendency to try to be more self-sufficient in food production and energy, and to be less dependent on traded commodities and traded manufactures. This will involve new development for declining and neglected areas in the industrialised countries, as it will for the poor countries. The long-term impact on international, as well as internal, patterns of trade and investment will be important. The present asymmetry of economic relationships between industrialised and developing countries will be reduced. This will be consistent with third world demands for a new international economic order.

Various factors will encourage this tendency towards greater self-sufficiency. First, income energy from the sun and income resources generated by continuing natural processes like plant growth tend to be more widely dispersed than deposits of fossil fuels and minerals. Second, the less developed countries are becoming increasingly reluctant to trade with the richer countries on disadvantageous terms, in commodities whose production displaces the production of food for themselves. Third, in the long run the costs of transport will continue to rise with rising energy costs. Fourth, the psychological appeal of greater self-sufficiency will become stronger, as people come to see it both as a way to reduce economic insecurity and dependence, and as a way of getting closer to nature and reality.

In a SHE economy greater self-reliance and local self-sufficiency will be connected with the growing importance of mutual aid and inter-reliance at the family, neighbourhood and local level. They will not mean greater selfishness. Nor will they mean greater isolation. In a SHE economy there will be less transport of goods between places, but more communication and travel between people.[49]

(5) *A More Decentralised Economy*

During the industrial age many towns and cities, districts and regions, in all the countries of Europe and North America became economically dependent on industries managed by the equivalent of absentee landlords — national or multi-national companies or national governments. Coal-mining and nickel-mining, steel-making, ship-building, automobiles and chemicals are a few examples of the many industries concerned. Localities like these are now coming face to face with the fact that decisions about the future of the industries on which they depend are right outside their control, and that those who run industries on that scale cannot give top priority to the interests of the people of the localities where they are situated. As the old industries decline, conventional economic thinking attempts to replace them by attracting comparable modern employment-creating industries from outside. But that simply replaces the old vulnerability with another of the same kind. A SHE economic path will take a different direction altogether. It will aim to develop greater local economic autonomy.

There will be two main approaches to this. The first will centre on local production to meet local needs. For example, more food and more energy for heat, light and power will be produced locally for local consumption. This will create local opportunities for work and result in money circulating locally instead of being spent elsewhere. The second approach will centre on local, small-scale ways of organising work — a bigger role for small businesses, local co-operatives and community enterprises, and bigger economic responsibilities for local (as compared with national) government agencies and local representative bodies.

(6) *'Another Development' Internationally*

The Business-As-Usual and HE scenarios envisage increasing international specialisation and the continuance of asymmetrical (more advanced/less advanced) economic relationships between industrialised and third world countries. According to this view, the rich countries must become even richer, in order to provide expanding markets for the products of poorer countries.

Conversely, the SHE path of development will lead the peoples of today's rich and poor countries to converge around an adequate and sustainable level of material consumption, to be achieved within twenty or thirty years from now. It will involve greater emphasis than today on the decentralised development of local self-reliance in rich countries and poor countries alike. In the rich countries it will involve a switch of emphasis towards personal and social development and quality of life. In the poorer countries it will involve recognising that effective development is self-development, to be achieved by helping people — both as individuals and in social groups — to acquire the skills and the wherewithal to develop better conditions for themselves, together with the confidence and the capacity to change their social and political structures if these are holding them back.

This bottom-up approach to development in third world countries has been called 'another development'. As I say, it contrasts with the conventional assumption that the further development of third world countries depends on the industrialised countries achieving more economic growth and thus being able to offer expanding markets for third world products. It also contrasts with the conventional top-down model of third world development which assumes that the transfer of capital-intensive technology from the industrialised world will generate wealth that will trickle down to the people.

On a SHE development path international economic activity will focus on the commonly shared objective that each country should be helped to become more self-reliant, not more dependent, economically. This will involve a more truly international approach to world economic development than the Business-As-Usual or HE scenarios envisage, with a new and important role for multi-national companies and a recognition that know-how and experience from third world countries may be relevant to the industrialised world.[51]

(7) Technology As Servant

Technology has been master during the industrial age. Technologies of super-human size — whether steel-mills, agricultural machines, or nuclear weapons — have dominated people. People have served machines as workers. As consumers, too, they have been ruled by the technological imperative: a new technology was possible, it had to be developed, and people had to be taught to want it and its products. In the HE scenario, technology would continue in the driving seat.

On the SHE path of development, we shall make technology our servant. We shall first think about people's needs, and then work out

41

what new or existing technologies are required to meet them. More effort will go into designing and producing machines and systems for individuals and small communities to use. These will help people to meet more of their own household and local needs for food and energy, for building and clothing, and for repairs and maintenance of every kind. As it happens, miniaturisation is the new frontier in many fields of technology now. Whereas the technologies of the industrial age drove productive activity out of the home and the neighbourhood into factories and offices controlled by remote employers and impersonal organisations, the new technologies of today — including especially, but by no means only, information technology — will help to bring it back under people's own control.

Many different terms have been used to describe benign technologies that serve human needs. 'Alternative', 'appropriate', 'humane', 'soft', 'intermediate' are among them. The key features of technology in a SHE economy are that it will be good to work with and under people's control, it will produce a good end product from which most people can benefit (not just a privileged minority), and it will be sparing in its use of resources and kind to the environment. This will apply in rich countries and poor alike. The idea that capital-intensive technology is appropriate for so-called advanced countries and intermediate technology for so-called developing countries will be regarded as nonsensical.

I must emphasise that the SHE path of development will not be hostile to technology. Because, in Britain especially, there has been opposition historically between the two cultures, science and technology on the one hand, arts and humanities on the other, it is sometimes assumed by conventional scientists, engineers and industrialists that the SHE vision of the future is anti-technology. Nothing could be further from the truth. It envisages the development and use of advanced technologies of every kind to help us along a saner, more humane and more ecological path of development than we have been following in the past.[52]

Who will decide what technologies to develop? Who will control their use? How can we make sure that technology enlarges people's capacities, instead of making people more dependent? These are the key questions about technology in a SHE society.

(8) *Town and Country*

On a SHE path of development, as economic activity becomes more self-sufficient and less centralised than today, the worldwide urbanisation of the industrial age will slow and go into reverse.

This has started to happen already in North America and Western Europe, where the number of people living in big cities has begun to decline and the number living in small towns has begun to rise. The trend towards megalopolis has already reached its limit in cities like London and New York. The cost of feeding, housing, maintaining and providing heat, light, power and transport for people in big cities will continue to go up. The advantages of their being there, as workers and consumers for the mass production industries typical of the industrial age, will continue to die away. There will be less and less satisfying employment and useful occupation for people in big cities as the high tide of the industrial age continues to ebb away.

The SHE vision of the future accepts this change of direction as inevitable, and foresees that more dispersed patterns of living and working will now develop. A sizeable rural resettlement movement is likely to emerge, with increasing emphasis on part-time farming and on the rejuvenation of rural communities. This will be consistent with more self-sufficiency and decentralisation, and in conflict with the further development of agribusiness farming. Space will become available in city centres for more convivial ways of life than industrialised society has permitted or than the HE scenario would allow. Urban food-growing will become commonplace. Millions of people in city, town and country will adopt new patterns of travel, transport, communication, shopping and entertainment.[53]

As the old urban, and especially inner city, economies continue to collapse, how will the millions of people trapped in them today be helped to extricate themselves? Efforts to revive those economies on conventional lines are unlikely to succeed. Eventually, of course, the problem, inherited from our industrial past, will ease as new, post-industrial patterns of growth take off and millions of people find ways of resettling themselves in the more dispersed, more self-reliant patterns of working and living that will be typical of the SHE future. But the transition will take twenty or thirty years, and many of the people most closely bound up in it will be those least able to cope. How are they to be helped? How is the transition to be eased?

(9) Greater Economic Equality

Industrial economies have justified inequalities of wealth and income, and therefore of resource consumption, on the ground that they motivate the abler and more energetic members of society to create more wealth for all. Those who make the cake bigger can be

43

rewarded with a bigger slice for themselves. Those who have more wealth provide markets for the goods and services, including labour, which other people want to sell.

This argument underlies the conventional approach to third world development today. True, the average North American already uses twice as much energy as the average Western European, and the average Western European six times as much as the average inhabitant of the third world. Nonetheless, according to the conventional argument, healthy development in the third world will depend on the rich countries of the North achieving even greater economic growth (and, therefore, an even higher consumption of energy and resources) so that they will provide bigger export markets for third world countries.

The SHE approach rejects that argument on the following grounds: the consumption of finite resources should be distributed more fairly; the expansion of trading relationships based on dominance and dependency is undesirable; and quality of life in the rich countries now requires a different path of development. A SHE future will be based on greater equality internally, as well as internationally, so that many more citizens can become economically more self-reliant, and all can enjoy a decent livelihood. A SHE society will perceive conspicuous material consumption as an outward symptom of inner insecurity, psychological weakness and spiritual poverty, as well as a social injustice and an ecological sin.

This change towards greater equality will not be brought about so much by a compulsory redistribution of wealth and income as by a change in attitudes.[54] Increasing numbers of people in the rich countries already understand that levels of material consumption and waste do not equate with standard of living or quality of life. They recognise that greater efficiency in the use of resources and cutting down on waste — for example, by switching to durable or repairable or recyclable products — need not reduce the standard of living offered by a throw-away society. They are also beginning to adopt simpler and more frugal ways of living, in a conscious move towards voluntary simplicity, sensing that to use an ever-increasing quantity of the planet's resources is not the most rewarding way to live, even from one's own point of view. Status symbols — symbols of success — are beginning to change accordingly.

These new attitudes are sometimes dismissed as middle-class and therefore, presumably, unimportant. This is a mistake, as we shall see in Chapter 6.

(10) *Work, Leisure and Life*

The contrast between the HE and SHE visions of the future is particularly marked here. In the HE scenario all the important work would be done by a minority of highly qualified experts. Everyone else would lead lives of leisure. Their leisure would be organised and catered for by managers and professionals in the booming leisure industries and leisure services. Precisely how these would be paid for has not yet been worked out by proponents of the HE future. What is clear is that the split between work and leisure that characterises the industrial economy would be accentuated.

By contrast, the SHE path of development will blur the split between work and leisure. Without going back to pre-industrial conditions, more people will live nearer to their work than in industrialised societies today, and their work will also be more closely integrated with other aspects of their lives. The boundaries between work and family, work and the local community, work and leisure, and paid work and unpaid work (like housework), will be less clear cut than in the industrial and hyper-industrial economies. More people will spend more of their time working in the informal sector of the economy where money is not the main measure of value. Fewer people will spend as much time as people spend today working for an employer in the labour market.

In a SHE economy people will be less willing to work at jobs which they perceive as personally frustrating or socially or ecologically damaging or futile; they will insist on spending their working time in ways that contribute to social wellbeing and their own personal goals and values. Men and women will share more equally the paid work they do for other people and the unpaid work they do for themselves, their families and their friends. The economic role of the family and the local community will acquire a new importance. The dividing line between economic and social activities and between economic and social policies — which has become increasingly sharp in the industrialised growth economy — will tend to fade.[9]

It is under this heading — work, leisure and life — that the significance of the informal economy is most clearly apparent. But the new relationship between informal and formal economic activity which it implies will affect every aspect of the SHE future. We turn to it now, in Chapter 3.

3
Walking on Two Legs

In Chapter 1 I suggested that overdeveloped institutional and intellectual structures are an important part of what is breaking down, and that personal experience and action are an important part of what should be encouraged to break through. A good example of overdeveloped structure is the formal economy based on money and jobs, and a good example of personal experience and action is the informal (gift and barter) economy of households and local communities. In Chapter 2 I suggested that the formal economy has reached the limits of its development in the industrialised countries. I also suggested that as we change direction towards a SHE economy the boundaries between work and family, work and the local community, work and leisure, paid work and unpaid work, will become less clear cut than in modern industrial societies. Informal economic activity will play a very much larger role.

Dual Economy: Formal and Informal

In this chapter I discuss this concept of a dual economy, divided into a formal part and an informal part.

The HE vision of post-industrial society ignores the informal economy altogether, and concentrates on the further development of the formal economy. The SHE vision perceives the formal economy to be in danger of collapse and finds the solution to this crisis in the revival of the informal economy. It holds out the prospect of a comparatively smooth transformation, instead of uncontrolled collapse and chaos, if people are helped to liberate themselves from their present degree of dependence on the formal economy and to develop more self-reliant, informal ways of providing for themselves and one another. Paradoxically, this process of decolonisation will create a new role for the formal economy, and help to restore its credibility. Creating the right relationship between the formal and informal sectors will be crucially important. The healthy development of each will depend on the healthy development of the other.

For many years development economists have known that third

46

world countries have dual economies. Those countries have a modern, westernised, money economy based on the towns and cities; and they have a traditional subsistence economy based on the rural villages in which money plays a much smaller part. But it is only within the last few years that people have begun to realise that the industrialised countries have a dual economy too. In years to come this concept of the dual economy, as applied to industrialised countries, may well be seen as the crucial breakthrough in late 20th century economic thinking. If the first edition of 'The Sane Alternative' achieved anything of importance, it was that it helped to make the concept of the dual economy more widely understood.[55]

So what is meant by the dual economy? The answer is very simple. As Figure 1 shows, the economy is divided into two parts. The formal part is shown above the horizontal line, the informal part below it.

The formal, *institutionalised part* of the economy is the part in which people work for money in jobs generated by the labour market; the goods they make and the services they provide are purchased for money or otherwise financed, for example by taxation. The *informal part* of the economy consists of the domestic or household sector and the neighbourhood or community sector. In this part of the economy the labour market does not operate (people don't have jobs), work is mainly unpaid (like housework), and goods and services are mainly given away or exchanged. The informal part of the economy is sometimes described as the gift and barter economy, as opposed to the money economy, though it also includes many unrecorded cash transactions.

Everyone lives, to a greater or lesser extent, in both parts of the dual economy. But in industrialised societies attention has been concentrated on the formal part of the economy, the part in which business corporations, government agencies and other organisations operate and in which individuals make and spend money. The prevailing concept of wealth has been of something created in the formal part of the economy by the 'economic' activities of industry and commerce and then spent, partly on the consumption of goods and services which people purchase from industry and commerce, and partly on the provision of 'social' wellbeing by public services. These public services have been financed as a spin-off from the economic activities of industry and commerce, which have therefore been seen as the 'wealth-creating' activities of society.

Representatives of different sectors of established opinion have continually argued about how the economy should work, and about

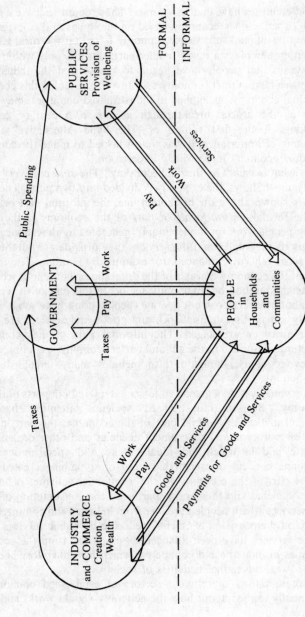

THE DUAL ECONOMY

PUBLIC SERVICES Provision of Wellbeing

GOVERNMENT

INDUSTRY and COMMERCE Creation of Wealth

PEOPLE in Households and Communities

FORMAL

INFORMAL

Work

Pay

Services

Public Spending

Taxes

Work

Pay

Taxes

Work

Pay

Goods and Services

Payments for Goods and Services

FIGURE 1

48

what changes should be made in various aspects of it. But they have all shared the prevailing assumption that the production of economic goods and the provision of social services by the formal part of the economy are the only kinds of economic activity that really matter. Economists and businesspeople, politicians and civil servants, trade unionists and bankers, have been concerned only with the kind of goods and services which cost money and with the kind of work which is done for an employer — jobs in the so-called labour market. Work which is done in the household or neighbourhood sectors, such as housework, have not counted in the employment statistics; and goods which are produced there, such as fruit and vegetables grown in gardens and allotments, have not counted in the Gross National Product (GNP).

The thrust of industrialisation, and the momentum it has developed in the past 200 years, has driven people increasingly out of the informal part of the economy into the formal part. In fact, this monetisation, institutionalisation and professionalisation of activities and aspects of life that people previously carried out for themselves and one another can be seen as the main hallmark of progress during the industrial age. The same pressure continues strong today. For example, single-parent mothers and fathers are encouraged to go out of their homes into jobs in the labour market, thus making the children dependent on institutionalised child care services. In general, men, women and children alike are encouraged to look outside the home for work, for the physical necessities of life, for teaching, for care, for entertainment. The process has been self-reinforcing, like the drift from public transport to private transport. As economic activity has shifted away from the home and local community, the home and local community have become less and less able to meet the economic and social needs of the people who still remain there, thus pushing them also into the money economy, the labour market and the organised social services. Until a few years ago, hardly anyone stopped to ask whether we would all be better off if we lived a greater proportion of our lives in the informal economy. The question of the right balance between the two halves of the dual economy hardly ever arose.

As I have said, the HE vision of the future ignores the existence of the informal economy. It assumes that even those activities that are still carried out by people for themselves — giving comfort to one another, for example, or even giving birth to children — will increasingly be taken over by professionals, or by institutions, or by machines. By contrast, a SHE path of development will reverse the hitherto prevailing shift out of informal into formal economic activity. More people will decide to spend a greater part of their time in the informal economy. They will find ways of reducing, rather than increasing, their dependence on money, jobs and social services provided by the formal economy.

So what kind of a process will this be, this reversal of institutionalisation in the economy? It will be a dual process, with two main aspects reinforcing one another. One aspect is that people will *liberate* themselves — to a greater or lesser extent — from dependence on the formal economy; they will develop their own alternative forms of economic activity in the informal economy. They will decide to do more of their work and more of their living in and around their households and local communities — to create use value rather than exchange value by their work. As more and more people decide to do this, they will create a growing movement towards greater economic self-reliance, alternative technologies, alternative health, rural resettlement, and so on. The other aspect is that people in responsible positions in the formal economy will consciously help to slim it down and manage its decline. People who work in the big organisations of government, business, finance, trade unions, public services, and the professions will increasingly see their role as helping other people (as well as themselves) to reduce their dependence on jobs, on money and on goods and services provided by industry, commerce, government and the public services. Increasingly they will aim to enable people — as citizens, customers, workers, patients, pupils and so on — to extend their autonomy and become more self-reliant. In thus helping others to liberate themselves, they will be *decolonising* the formal economy as if it were an over-extended empire which needs to be run down. They will do this, no doubt, in many cases because they see the writing on the wall, rather than of their own free choice.

Five years ago, when I was writing the first edition of this book, I had to admit that most people involved in business strategy and public policy would not yet find it easy to relate ideas like these to their own concerns. That is no longer true. The management of contraction has now become a fact of every-day life in business and public service.

Of course, if you listened only to politicians, industrialists and trade union leaders on public platforms you might think that little had changed. The so-called 'opinion-formers' still seem to be primarily concerned with questions about the formal economy. Should

50

government have more control over industry or less? Should nationalised industries be 'privatised', i.e. commercialised and handed over to big business? Should trade unions be cut down to size or given more power? Is it more important that inflation or unemployment should be reduced? Should government borrowing and spending go up or down? Should public services like education, health and welfare be expanded or should they be commercialised and pruned back? Questions like these, that ignore the existence of the informal economy and the possibility of its playing a bigger role, still dominate the political and economic discussions that take place in public and in the press.

But below the surface there has been a big change in attitude and outlook. Privately, many politicians and business people are much less sure of the old conventional answers than they were five years ago. More important, they are beginning to doubt whether they have been asking the right questions. This is true not only in Britain, but in every other industrialised country too. How has this change come about?

Formal Economy: Background

The decades leading up to the late 1970s saw tremendous development in the size and organisation of the 'wealth-creating' part of the formal economy. Take Britain as an example.

First, there was increasing concentration in the business system itself.[56] In 1935 half of the manufacturing sector's output was produced by the 800 biggest companies, in 1958 by the 420 biggest, in 1970 by the 140 biggest, and the merger mania of the early 'seventies further increased this process of concentration.

Second, and equally important, was the increasing concentration of power in other economic institutions outside the business system, i.e. in government, trade unions and finance, and the drift towards a centralised corporate state.

By the late 'seventies the government controlled a greater proportion of British business than ever before — nationalised either by deliberate policy or as the only way to rescue otherwise bankrupt industries. Other forms of government intervention in the business system had grown continually too. Legislation protecting employees, investors, consumers and the public, and also legislation aimed at making industry more efficient, hedged the business enterprise on all sides. Through the 1960s and the 1970s the government continually increased its financial help to industry — the high technology industries like aerospace and computers no less than the older

51

industries in difficulty like shipbuilding and motorcars. Government intervened to restructure industry by promoting mergers. Continuing government efforts were made in various ways to develop machinery and procedures for economic and industrial planning, and for prices and incomes control, in consultation with industry, the trade unions and finance.

The trade unions had also grown bigger and more powerful. Between 1960 and 1974 the number of unions with 100,000 members or more grew from 17 to 25, and their total membership from $6\frac{1}{2}$ million to 9 million, while the total number of unions dropped from 664 to 488. The trade union movement in Britain remained fragmented, compared with certain other countries like Germany. But the successful development of collective bargaining had led to greater and greater participation in economic decision-making by the trade union movement at every level. The 1974 Labour Government's 'social contract' with the trade unions was central to its economic policy, and the trade unions participated fully in formulating the government's industrial strategy.

The financial institutions, similarly, had grown bigger and more powerful. The figures show that personal shareholdings in large companies dropped significantly between 1963 and 1975, while the holdings of institutions (insurance companies, pension funds, banks, nominee companies, and charities and non-profit bodies) rose correspondingly. As the Diamond Royal Commission[57] put it in 1975, 'What seems to have been happening is that individuals as a group have been turning away from direct investment in industry and placing their savings with pension funds, life insurance companies, unit trusts, etc., which in turn invest them in industry.'

So big business, big government, big trade unions and big financial institutions had all become more powerful. They had also become more remote from the people whom they were meant to serve and the people who worked in them. But more than that. They had also come closer together in forums like the National Economic Development Council. They now combined in a governing economic elite.

This development was seen by many as a sign that economic democracy was beginning to take its place alongside the kind of political democracy which began with the American and French Revolutions two hundred years ago. Some, taking a longer historical perspective, saw it as a sign that economic activity, having emerged as a separate department of life following the Renaissance and the Reformation, was now converging again — at least at the national

52

level — with the social and political domains. A 'decline of business civilisation' was taking place, said Robert Heilbroner.[27] A 'new ideology' was emerging, said George C. Lodge,[58] which would transform the relationship between business and society.

In the early 1970s my own view of what had happened at the national level was that it was more like the emergence of a corporate state than of economic democracy. But I was one of many who hoped that a way forward would be found by changing the formal responsibilities of business enterprises and financial institutions, so that they would be obliged to serve all their stakeholders (including their employees and customers) and no longer treat the interests of their shareholders as paramount. I argued that this change at the level of the enterprise, together with more open procedures for deciding government policies on taxation, interest rates, public borrowing and public spending, would lead to an efficient 'non-profit' economy. Economic democracy would then be based on the representation in economic decision-making of all the main interested parties, both at the national level and at the level of the enterprise.[59]

This was one of several approaches to democratising the structures of the formal economy which were canvassed at that time in a number of countries, with the aim of making it operate more fairly and more efficiently. They did not succeed. They were overtaken by political changes. For example, in Britain and the United States the new right-wing Thatcher and Reagan governments misinterpreted the prevailing hostility to big government and big trade unions as a vote of confidence in big business and the commercial way of life. In any case, the idea of economic democracy had little attraction for top industrialists, financiers, trade union leaders, politicians or public officials; it threatened the unaccountable powers which they all now enjoyed in economic affairs.

Most importantly, though, the steady drift over many years towards size and centralisation had generated such a backlash against all the big institutions which now dominated people's lives, and such a sense of remoteness from them, that no-one apart from a few committed reformers had much interest in restructuring them or thought the effort worthwhile. That intuitive judgment, I now believe, was quite correct. The first priority is not to reform the formal economy but to disengage from it before it breaks down completely. Partial disengagement will be a prior condition for effective reform.

Formal Economy: International Perspective
Nonetheless, the structure of the formal economy — that is the way

53

in which various economic institutions interrelate and the power which they exercise towards one another and the people with whom they deal — is an important part of the background against which this larger change will take place. It has differed greatly from country to country.

For example, take the trade unions. In Britain the trade unions have always been socialist in ideology. In politics they have been allied with one of the two governing parties of the last half century. In the 1970s they were the government's partners in the 'social contract', deeply involved in economic policy at the national level. But within the enterprise they retained the old conception of their role as adversaries to management. This meant that, unlike the trade unions in Germany for example, they were unwilling to take on a share of responsibility for the success of the enterprise and to become full partners in it. So, in the 1970s in Britain, the prospect of introducing greater economic democracy in the formal economy was dominated by the trade unions and confused because of the conflict between their partner and adversary roles.[60]

In the United States, on the other hand, the trade unions have always been robustly capitalist — adversaries to management only in the sense of wanting a bigger share of the fruits of the capitalist system. There has been no question of the trade unions partnering a socialist government, because state socialism has never been on the agenda in the United States. So pressures for economic democracy in the United States have come not from the trade unions but from the minority group, environmental and consumerist lobbies like Nader's raiders, from wider share-ownership and profit-sharing schemes like Louis Kelso's employee stock option programmes (ESOP),[61] and from what Peter Drucker[62] described as pension fund socialism. 'Social responsibility' has always been the big challenge to management in the United States, 'participation' in Britain.

Now take the financial institutions. In Britain and the United States they have traditionally been based on financial markets like the Stock Exchange, though in Britain the big banks and other financial institutions have now become more dominant than they were. In both these countries people working in the financial sector have been concerned primarily with the management of money (i.e. making money out of money) rather than with the management of industry. In Germany, on the other hand, the financial sector has been dominated by the big banks, which have been much more concerned than in Britain and the United States with the successful management of

54

industry. In France the financial sector has been dominated by banks and other financial institutions as in Germany, but the most important institutions have been nationalised. These differences have significantly affected the way the formal economy has operated in these four countries.

When we come to economic planning, we find that the French tradition of strong central government has facilitated the development of continuing, organised arrangements for economic planning. In the USA, on the other hand, where strong central government has always been traditionally anathema, national economic planning has hardly existed. Britain used to come half way between France and the United States: economic planning was never completely ruled out but was always fitful and half-hearted. In Japan, as in France, economic planning was more successful. But in Japan, as compared with France, the role of government tended to be more limited. By coordinating different interests it helped a consensus to develop. But unlike the French government it could not exercise real leadership, except when this arose from a consensus with business leaders.

The role of the elites has been another feature in which the formal economy has differed from country to country. In Britain the economic elites have been separated and static: people have generally made a career in politics, the civil service, industry or the City, and have remained in one of these. Personal links and mobility between politics, the civil service, industry and the City have been rare. In France, by contrast, there has existed something more like a single elite of people who have known each other since they started their careers together in the Grandes Ecoles, and who have circulated between government, industry, finance and politics. The United States has come somewhere between Britain and France in this respect. Leading people have circulated readily through business, government and finance; but, partly for geographical reasons, they have not constituted a single centralised elite, based on the capital city.

Many other factors have played an important part in shaping the formal economy in each particular country. For example, Britain's economic system has evolved more or less uninterruptedly over the past century or so. In the United States also the economic system has evolved uninterruptedly since the Civil War, but greater modernity and wider frontiers have allowed more rapid change than in Britain. In Germany and Japan on the other hand, the destruction of industrial plant and economic institutions in the second world war meant that in many respects a new start was necessary and possible in 1945.

The way in which the formal economy has developed has also been affected by the general climate of opinion towards the business community. In Britain influential sections of society have always been anti-business, going back to the churches, universities, armed forces, learned professions and rural gentry of the 18th and 19th centuries. In Germany on the other hand, pro-business sentiment has always been stronger, while in the United States the business of business has been the business of America. In the United States today business leadership still seems to take initiatives, whereas in Britain business leaders have been on the defensive for many years.

When we look beyond the western industrialised economies, larger differences in the structure of formal economies come into the picture. Some countries have centralised economies, in the sense that the main economic decisions are taken centrally, while others have decentralised economies in the sense that individual enterprises have a great deal of freedom to pursue their own policies. Some economies are predominantly capitalist, in the sense that the investor interest is paramount; others are predominantly socialist, in the sense that state ownership and control is paramount; in others, as in Yugoslavia, worker-managed enterprises predominate; theoretically, other economies might be dominated by municipal or consumer enterprises (i.e. by businesses owned by the local community or by their customers); and many countries have a 'mixed economy', containing a mixture of these various types of enterprise.

These different structures of the formal economy have been reflected in the different political ideologies of the industrial age. The most important of these ideologies have been market capitalism, corporate statism, and state socialism (sometimes called state capitalism) — broadly coinciding with right, centre and left on the conventional political spectrum. (The Jeffersonian ideology — corresponding to a decentralised free market of small producers and consumers — and the various 19th century forms of decentralised socialist thinking — corresponding to an economy based on producer, consumer and community co-operatives — were marginalised by the drift to size and centralisation of the later industrial age. These, and the later ideas of such people as Rudolf Steiner, Henry George, G. K. Chesterton and the Social Credit movement, are likely to become increasingly relevant from now on).

Throughout the consensus years of continuing economic growth, say between 1950 and 1975, it was widely supposed by knowledgeable people that in due course most countries would

56

develop some kind of mixed economy. This would contain the best features of various countries' systems and would represent a balance between market capitalism and state socialism mediated by the consultative arrangements of the corporate state. It was thus assumed that in time the formal economies of East and West — including Soviet Russia and the United States — would become more like each other. The old ideological conflict between capitalism and communism would fade into pragmatic differences about which formal economic arrangements worked best in this circumstance or that.

This comfortable consensus was shaken when the growth years came to an end. As the formal economy ceased to function satisfactorily in many countries, political opinion became more sharply divided. In Britain, for example, the Thatcher Conservatives committed themselves to restoring market capitalism, the Labour left began to call for full-blooded state socialism, and a new centre grouping of Liberals and Social Democrats sought to recover and strengthen the consensus politics of the 1950s and '60s. Each of these three minority opinions claimed that it had the secret of restoring a well-functioning formal economy. However, the majority of the population were doubtful if any of these approaches would succeed.

The majority was intuitively right. The fact is that in all the industrialised countries — East as well as West — the formal economy has developed byond its limit, to the point where, having deprived people of the capacity and the expectation of doing things for themselves and one another, it can no longer organise them to work and provide the goods and services that it has taught them to demand. In all the industrialised countries, East and West, the formal economy is now best understood as an overextended empire nearing the point of collapse. The most important question common to all these countries is whether their formal economy will actually break down, or whether they can decolonise it voluntarily in good order before the breakdown comes. Decolonising the formal economy means creating conditions which enable people to work, produce and care for themselves and one another much more than they can today.

The Future of the Welfare State

The shift away from informal into formal activity has not applied only to productive activity or, as the industrial age has called it, the creation of wealth. It has applied equally to caring activity or, as the industrial age has called it, the provision of welfare. This shift out of informal into formal activity has led to a wide separation between the way industrialised societies create wealth and the way they provide welfare. The creation of wealth is regarded as the task of the business and industry sector, and the provision of welfare as the task of the public services sector.

This way of thinking about and organising productive activity and caring activity has meant that the growth of social welfare has had to depend on the growth of economic prosperity, which has therefore always had to be given priority. 20th century socialists have shared this assumption with 19th century radical capitalists. Just as the latter assumed in the 1830s that solutions to the 'condition of England' question depended on the stimulus to economic activity that free trade and retrenchment of government spending would provide, so contemporary socialists[63] have assumed that economic growth was an essential prerequisite to increasing social welfare. The same, of course, is true of U.S. multinational business tycoons and Soviet state planners today.

In the 1950s and '60s mature industrial societies seemed to most people to be progressing more or less satisfactorily according to these assumptions. But this was not long sustained. On the one hand the limits to economic growth began to close in, while on the other the demand for social welfare services — fed by their availability at public expense, by widening perceptions of the scale of social need that ought to be met, by the vested interest of the growing number of social service professionals, and by the general readiness of politicians to offer more — began to escalate. The industrial growth engine turned, in a few short years, from a miracle machine capable of meeting continually growing needs, into a disaster device programmed to generate aspirations which it could not possibly fulfil — and programmed, moreover, to stunt people's capacity to fulfil their aspirations for themselves.

Conventional politicians of all shades today (including right-wing Conservatives who believe in the invisible hand of the market economy, left-wing Labour socialists who believe in the omnicompetence of a benign state, and those in between — Social Democrats, Liberals and 'wet' Conservatives — who believe in a mixed economy) still cling to the industrial paradigm. They continue to assume that economic recovery on conventional lines can provide for further expansion of social services on conventional lines, and the main arguments between them are about how economic recovery is to be achieved and how social services should be paid for. They will continue to voice this basic set of assumptions, though with declining conviction and credibility, until they are provided with a new set of assumptions to succeed it. To articulate that new set of assumptions coherently and clearly is one of the most important tasks of the present creative, pre-political phase of the transition to post-industrial society.

This task is well under way in the field of health. Instead of debating endlessly what is the best way of providing an ever increasing range and volume of conventional treatments for ill-health — privately, publicly or by a supposedly efficient mixture of the two — many people are turning their attention to quite different questions.

Some are developing alternative therapies. These include therapies based on good diet and on tackling the psychosomatic aspects of ill-health. This approach will almost certainly yield more effective — and, in due course, less costly — results, for instance in many cancer cases, than are given by today's conventional treatments based on surgery, radiotherapy and drugs. Others recognise that what we are accustomed to call health services should really be called sickness services. Sickness services cannot reasonably be expected to make much positive contribution to people's good health. The need is for new approaches that actually can help people to live healthier lives in a healthier society. We have to ask how people can be helped to help themselves — whether as individuals, or as groups of fellow-sufferers with the same health problem, or as local communities. How can people be helped to cope, and to help one another to cope, with their illnesses and disabilities? How can they be helped to create a healthier way of life and a healthier environment to live in? How can they be helped to become less dependent for their health on the drug industry, the medical profession, and the established health care services? The growing emphasis on health education and the self-help health movement reflects this approach. So does the growing emphasis on community health.

These new initiatives in health are to be found in every country in the western industrialised world. They stem from doubt whether a business-as-usual approach to the provision of health and medical care will be feasible for much longer. They add up to a new approach to health care based on the growth of a greatly expanded 'informal economy' for health, emphasising self-reliance and mutual aid instead of dependence on professionalised services, and empowering all citizens to create healthier conditions of life for themselves. This would go hand in hand with a streamlined formal sector of efficient, up-to-date hospitals and professional medical service available to all.

Together, an expanded informal sector and a streamlined formal sector can make up a well-balanced dual economy for health.[64]

Restructuring the Economy

Returning now to the future of the economy as a whole, the first priority will be to liberate ourselves from our present degree of dependence on the formal economy and to generate a revival of informal economic activity. But we shall still need to keep the national and international perspective in view. So how is the structure of economic institutions likely to change?

In his study of business civilisation in decline, Robert Heilbroner[27] concluded that the demise of the business system is likely to proceed by degrees, insensibly altering a civilisation that can be called 'capitalist' into one that, whatever we decide to call it, will be very different. Heilbroner envisages a tightly controlled society in which the traditional pillars of capitalism — the legitimacy of private property and the operation of the market mechanism 'have been amended beyond recognition, if not wholly superseded by state property and state directives.' In the more distant future, Heilbroner finds it possible to imagine an eventual dissolution of centralised power. But he does not think this can possibly occur for a long time to come. Heilbroner, living in capitalist America as does J. K. Galbraith, perceives as does Galbraith[65] that capitalism is being superseded, and that this means a greater involvement by the state in economic matters. What North American thinkers do not find it so easy to perceive as we who have lived through the last thirty years in countries like Britain, France and Sweden, is that the practical limits to centralised state control are quickly reached, and that decentralisation then becomes necessary.

Norman Macrae believes that decentralisation rather than further centralisation of economic activity will and should take place. In a survey seven years ago[66] on the coming entrepreneurial revolution, Macrae forecast that the age of big business corporations is probably drawing to its end; these institutions may now be past their peak; during the next two or three decades they may virtually disappear in their present form. They will not, in Macrae's view, be replaced by state capitalism; indeed, many services now provided by government will be returned to competitive private enterprise. Incentives to make workers happier will be individually designed, so as to allow everyone to choose their own lifestyles. Dynamic corporations of the future will try several alternative ways of doing things in competition within themselves. The role of their workers, as individuals or as group co-operatives, will be as entrepreneurial sub-contractors. In Macrae's words, successful big corporations will have developed themselves into confederations of entrepreneurs.

It now seems less likely than it did to many people like Heilbroner and Galbraith a few years ago, that the economy of the future will be dominated by the State. It now seems more likely that small enterprises, including co-operatives, community businesses and Macrae's decentralised confederations of entrepreneurial groups, will play a larger part in the economy. But this decentralisation should be seen as only one element in a more complex series of changes that is now under way.

Figure 2 outlines the unifying perspective in which these changes — including the coming revival of the informal economy — should be seen. It shows that change is taking place in two dimensions simultaneously. First, as shown on the left-hand side of the diagram, a process is taking place which I have called 'dismantling the nation state.'[11] We are moving out of an age dominated by sovereignty at the level of the nation state, and into an age in which the vital role of self-government is recognised at various different levels. Second, as shown on the right-hand side of the diagram, politics is converging with economics.

In this perspective, the economic dimension of democracy is seen to take many forms. At one end of the spectrum it includes measures like the drawing up and administering of codes of conduct by the United Nations to govern the behaviour of multinational companies. At the other end it involves a more equal sharing of paid and unpaid work between men and women in the individual household. Economic democracy also applies at every intermediate point on the spectrum, in forms appropriate to each. For example, in many countries local government authorities which formerly had few economic functions have been taking on increasing responsibilities connected with the local economy and local employment.

The future structure of economic activity is likely to reflect this growing awareness that true economic democracy must mean much more than changes in the institutional balance of power at the national level and at the level of the business enterprise. Economic democracy implies a new balance of functions and power, i.e. a new social and political balance, at every level. This new balance of functions and power will be an important structural feature of the permanently sustainable economy of the future; and, at the basic level of the household and local community, it will be directly connected with a

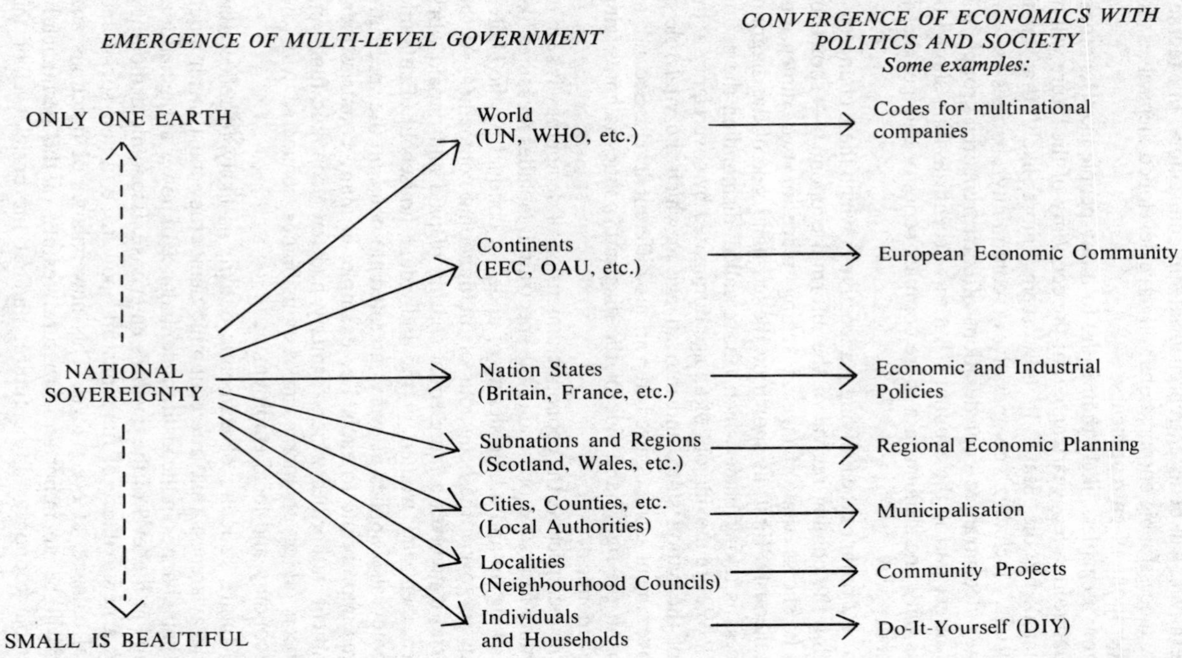

EMERGENCE OF MULTI-LEVEL GOVERNMENT

World
(UN, WHO, etc.)

Continents
(EEC, OAU, etc.)

Nation States
(Britain, France, etc.)

Subnations and Regions
(Scotland, Wales, etc.)

Cities, Counties, etc.
(Local Authorities)

Localities
(Neighbourhood Councils)

Individuals
and Households

ONLY ONE EARTH ← - - - - NATIONAL SOVEREIGNTY - - - - → SMALL IS BEAUTIFUL

CONVERGENCE OF ECONOMICS WITH
POLITICS AND SOCIETY

Some examples:

Codes for multinational
companies

European Economic Community

Economic and Industrial
Policies

Regional Economic Planning

Municipalisation

Community Projects

Do-It-Yourself (DIY)

FIGURE 2

new balance between formal and informal economic activity.

In this chapter, by looking at the economy whole, with its formal and informal parts together, we can see that the future structure of economic activity will be shaped in two main ways. It will be shaped partly by the momentum of the changes which have been taking place in the formal structure of economic institutions. Those changes have been made — in different ways in different countries according to differences in their culture and history — in response to political and social changes generated in the past. They have tended to point, at least in certain limited senses, towards greater democracy in economic affairs. But from now on developments in the structure of economic activity will increasingly be shaped not only by the push of the past, but also by the pull of a new vision of the future. This will involve: recognition of the need to achieve a sustainable world economy within the next 30 years; the rising aspiration of increasing numbers of people to become less dependent on jobs and money and goods and services of the consumer society; and awareness that the institutionalised economy has reached its limits.

The pull of this new vision of the future will require a change of direction, a shift of balance — as if we were a person walking forward at the point where it is time to shift our balance from one leg to the other.

Progress during the industrial age has been made by organising and formalising, monetising and professionalising, human activities of every kind. What comes next?

The HE vision of the future requires us to continue further in this same direction with accelerating speed. If we do this, we risk — like any walker proceeding in this fashion — falling flat on our face. The resulting two-class society, sharply split between a dependent majority of idle and poor consumers and clients, and a controlling minority of hard-working but privileged producers, professionals, managers and experts, could never be stable.

The SHE vision, by contrast, perceives that a shift of balance is now necessary — away from formal, impersonally organised activities to informal, inter-personal ways of living and working. This is the direction in which, in the period of time now beginning, the most important new forms of economic growth and social progress will be achieved.

Many new practical tasks face us as we begin to take this new direction into the future. At the personal level these will involve learning to do many things for ourselves and other people which we

63

have become incapable of doing during the industrial age. For society as a whole, the new tasks will focus on helping a benign dual economy to emerge out of the current crisis of the industrial way of life. By a benign dual economy I mean the economic arrangements for a fair, well-integrated society, in which all citizens participate and live their lives on equal terms in both the formal and the informal economy. Such a benign dual economy will contrast with another possible kind of dual economy — the divisive dual economy of a two-tier society whose superior and more fortunate members monopolise the activities of the formal economy and exclude the rest of us from it.

4
A Shift of Paradigms

We have seen that, if we are to move towards a sane, humane, ecological (SHE) future, we shall have to change the direction which modern society has been taking. We have suggested what this will imply in the economic sphere. In the following chapter we shall suggest that this change of direction can be seen as a transformation.

In this chapter we discuss paradigm shifts. They will be an essential part of the required change of direction, or transformation. We describe what they are; we consider briefly how they might affect the meaning of concepts like *wealth, power* and *growth;* we then look a little more closely at the possibility of a shift in the prevailing paradigm of *work,* with particular attention to the way in which the transition might be made from the present paradigm to a new one; and we conclude by noting the practical need to foster and accelerate paradigm shifts of this kind.

What Is A Paradigm Shift?

A paradigm shift is the change that takes place from time to time in a basic belief or assumption (or in a constellation of basic beliefs or assumptions) underlying our perceptions and actions. It can be seen as the cultural equivalent of an evolutionary leap. A well known example is the shift, which took place in the 16th and 17th centuries and is associated with the names of Copernicus and Galileo, from the view that the sun goes round the earth to the view that the earth goes round the sun.

The concept of a paradigm shift arose from studies of the history of science. It was given currency by T. S. Kuhn in his book on 'The Structure of Scientific Revolutions'.[67] Kuhn examined 'the major turning points in scientific development associated with the names of Copernicus, Newton, Lavoisier, and Einstein. More clearly than most other episodes in the history of at least the physical sciences, these display what all scientific revolutions are about. Each of them necessitated the community's rejection of one time-honoured scientific theory in favour of another incompatible with it. Each produced a consequent shift in the problems available for scientific scrutiny and in the standards by which the profession determined what should count as an admissible problem or as a legitimate problem-solution. And each transformed the scientific imagination in ways that we shall ultimately need to describe as a transformation of the world within which scientific work was done. Such changes, together with the controversies that almost always accompany them, are the defining characteristics of scientific revolutions.'

Kuhn concluded that 'the successive transition from one paradigm to another via revolution is the actual developmental pattern of mature science. . . When an individual or group first produces a synthesis able to attract most of the next generation's practitioners, the older schools gradually disappear. In part, their disappearance is caused by their members' conversion to the new paradigm. But there are always some men who cling to one or another of the old views, and they are simply read out of the profession which thereafter ignores their work.' The prevailing paradigm provides the agenda for all the ongoing activities of routine practitioners of science. As the paradigm shift occurs, those activities change their direction in accordance with the new paradigm.

In very much the same way as Kuhn described for science, prevailing paradigms provide the context for routine activity in non-scientific affairs, and shifts take place from one paradigm to another. For example, human beings can see themselves as outside nature, whence they can observe it, dominate it and exploit it; or, by contrast, they can feel themselves to be an integral part of nature. One aspect of the change of direction to the SHE future will be a shift from the first of these two paradigms to the second i.e. from a scientific and economic view of nature to an ecological and spiritual view. Again, the dominant paradigm in economic affairs may be one of maximising and expansion; or it may be one of sufficiency and balance. A shift from the first to the second of these two paradigms will also be part of the transition to the SHE future.

In general, the paradigm shifts associated with the transition to the SHE future will reflect a shift of emphasis away from the overdeveloped, structured, exterior aspects of life towards the underdeveloped, unstructured, interior aspects — for example,

from	to
scientific and academic knowledge	intuitive understanding
representative politics and bureaucratic government	community politics and direct democracy

from	*to*
the institutional economy based on money and jobs	the gift and barter economy of households and local communities
an arm's length relationship between professionals and their clients	personally shared experience
institutionalised social services	caring personal relationships
organised religious activity and codified religious doctrines	personal spiritual experience

Key ideas in these six cases include: knowledge and learning; power and public service; wealth and work; teaching and healing; welfare and care; religious ministry and spiritual communion. In every case the prevailing paradigm can be expected to shift in much the same way: the acquisition of externally validated credentials, positions, possessions and qualifications which give one an advantage over one's less successful fellows will come to seem less important; the development of personal capacities to live one's life under one's own control, and also to help one's fellows to do the same, will come to seem more important.

One possible way of looking at these changes is to say that knowledge, power, wealth, etc. will come to be thought less desirable in themselves than we have hitherto supposed; and that thinking them desirable may become an obstacle to the good life. This corresponds to the ascetic element in much religious teaching: what the world calls good is actually bad, and for the good of our souls we should forswear it. But that is too hard for most people. An easier approach is to say that knowledge, power, wealth, etc. will continue to represent positive human aspirations; but to reinterpret what they mean.

Wealth

The first of two examples of rethinking about wealth is a letter of mine, published in the London 'Times' on 16th February 1977.

'Lord Plowden (Letters, February 11) believes that the important thing for this country which should take precedence over anything else, is the creation of more wealth; that it is industry and commerce that create this wealth; and that from this wealth will flow new jobs, welfare and education. Most other leading people in industry, politics, trade unions, civil service and the media in Britain today still seem to share this view.

Fortunately, a great many others among us do not. We question the idea of "wealth" as something created by manufacturers of cigarettes and sweets, but not by doctors and dentists; created by bankers and commercial lawyers, but not by housewives and social workers; created by agribusiness, but not by people working their smallholdings, allotments and gardens; created by advertising agencies, but not by schools; created by the arms trade, but not by the peacepeople. Is it a law of nature that compels us to make more and more *things,* including many that are harmful or useless, before we can attend to the needs of *people?*

No, it is not. The idea of wealth as something that has to be created by the "economic" activities of industry and commerce, so that it can then be spent on something quite different called "social" wellbeing, is part of the metaphysic of the industrial age. As that age draws towards its end, one of this country's greatest strengths is the great number among its people who already sense that the old metaphysic is out of date.

We, who live in the first industrial country, are now among the first to arrive at the next great turning point in history. We should take heart. In our intuitive wisdom, we are already laying the foundations for the post-industrial future, in spite of the chorus of influential voices like Lord Plowden's that urge us vainly to prolong the industrial past.'

The second is an extract from an unpublished paper called 'The New Wealth', in which Tom Burke, formerly director of Friends of the Earth in London, suggested what wealth might mean in future.

'The new wealth might count as affluent the person who possessed the necessary equipment to make the best use of natural energy flows to heat a home or warm water — the use which accounts for the bulk of an individual's energy demand. The symbols of this kind of wealth would not be new cars, TVs or whatever, although they would be just as tangible and just as visible. They would be solar panels, insulated walls or a heat pump.

The poor would be those who remained dependent on centralised energy distribution services, vulnerable to interruption by strike, malfunction or sabotage, and even more vulnerable to rising tariffs set by inaccessible technocrats themselves the victims of market forces beyond their control. The new rich would boast not of how new their television was but of how long it was expected to last and

68

how easy it would be to repair.

Wealth might take the form of ownership of, or at least access to, enough land to grow a proportion of one's food. This would reduce the need to earn an ever larger income in order to pay for increasingly expensive food. Wealth would consist in having access to most goods and services within easy walking or cycling distance of home thus reducing the need to spend more time earning more money to pay for more expensive transport services. A high income would be less a sign of wealth than of poverty since it would indicate dependence on the provision by someone else of a job and a workplace in order to earn the income to rent services. Wealth would consist in having more control over the decisions that affected wellbeing and in having the time to exercise that control.'

The emergence of a new paradigm of wealth as suggested by Burke will depend very largely on the practical activities of people who, in the way they live their lives, recognisably create new forms of economic and social wellbeing for themselves and others. At the same time, there is a real need for imaginative discussion and speculation about what might be meant by wealth in a sane, humane, ecological future — what would be meant by a wealthy person, a wealthy community, the creation of wealth, a rich life, poverty, and so on? How could the shift, already evident in the voluntary simplicity movement, be accelerated from today's prevailing paradigm of wealth to the new one? How did comparable shifts in the meaning of wealth occur at times like the industrial revolution, and the Renaissance and the Reformation?

Power

In an earlier book[11] I suggested that the prevailing concept of power has evolved from the crudely primitive to the institutionally and metaphysically complex, and that it is now due to evolve further — towards the idea of power as the interior capacity of persons and groups of persons to control their own lives and to contribute creatively to the lives of others. In other words, the new power will be seen as the absence of dependence, and as the ability to help others to shake off dependence.

The dependence of women in a patriarchal society can be seen as a model which applies to most citizens, consumers, workers, patients, pupils and other clients of the political, managerial and professional establishment in modern industrial societies. Here is how the Boston Women's Health Book Collective came to see the situation.

'Talking to each other, we realised that many of us shared a common perception of men — that they all seemed to be able to turn themselves on and to do things for themselves. We tended to feel passive and helpless and to expect and need men to do things for us. We were trained to give our power over to men. We had reduced ourselves to objects. We remained children, helpless and giving other people power to define us and objectify us. As we talked together, we realised that one of our central fantasies was our wish to find a man who could turn us on, do for us what we could not do for ourselves, make us feel alive and affirm our existence. It was as if we were made of clay and men would mould us, shape us, and bring us to life. This was the material of our childhood dreams: "Some day my prince will come". We were always disappointed when men did not accomplish this impossible task for us. And we began to see our passive, helpless ways of handing power over to others as crippling to us. What became clear to us was that we had to change our expectations for ourselves. There was no factual reason why we could not assert and affirm our own existence to do and act for ourselves.'[68]

Just as these women felt they had been trained to give their power to other people to define them, so we, in Britain and in other over-institutionalised countries, are conditioned to give our power to employers and governments and the mass media. The concept of non-violent power, of people's capacity to act for themselves, of sovereignty peacefully welling up from all the people, is relevant for us all.

This concept of non-violent power is likely to be central to the politics of a sane, humane, ecological tomorrow. When I was writing the first edition of this book five years ago, the Northern Ireland Peace People, founded by Mairead Corrigan and Betty Williams, offered a good example of an attempt to develop and to exercise this kind of power. As I write the revised edition, the women's peace movement in Britain is offering a similar example. As with all human endeavours, these initiatives will often fail to achieve their stated goals. Nonetheless, as the old political order and the credibility of industrial-age politics break down, movements of this kind are helping to create new forms of politics for a post-industrial age. They herald a coming upsurge in non-violent community politics — the politics of the volunteer — which may bypass the blockages in the existing political system and help us to break through to new patterns of political stability.

Two points are important. The first is that, instead of seeking to overpower the adversary, the non-violent approach seeks to withdraw power from the adversary. Less powerful people are less powerful, partly because they have been conditioned to give power to more powerful people and organisations. The non-violent approach seeks to develop the capacity of the less powerful to withdraw that power, to act freely for themselves and to control their own lives. The second is that this approach goes much wider and is much more radically transformative than the kind of extra-parliamentary direct political action recommended by overtly political groups. The latter hope to use non-violent (and sometimes violent) direct action as an instrument of protest and pressure which will influence national political goals and the processes of the state. The non-violent transformative approach, on the other hand, is about people developing the power to change for themselves the actual ways and conditions in which they live and work. It is about people taking power, not so much to influence the glamorous, artificial sphere of conventional politics and government, as to do their own real politics and to govern their own real lives for themselves.

The emergence of the new paradigm of power, as of wealth, will depend very largely on the practical activities of people who, in the way they live their lives, recognisably create new forms of power for themselves and recognisably help others to do the same. Practical training and experience in the exercise of non-violent power will play an important part. At the same time, there is a real need for imaginative and speculative discussion about what might be meant by power in a sane, humane, ecological society. Peter Cadogan's 'Direct Democracy'[55] is a good example of what is wanted here. So is 'The Price of Peace'[69] by Ciaran McKeown of the Peace People in Northern Ireland. Jim Cairns, former Deputy Prime Minister of Australia, is a politician of national standing whose thinking points in this direction.[70]

Growth

The concept of growth will continue, I am sure, to play a vital part in our thinking. But what kinds of growth shall we value? What kinds of growth shall we try to avoid? When, and in what circumstances, shall we prefer balance or stability to growth? As we move into the SHE future, the growth paradigm may be expected to shift from the present emphasis on tangible, impersonal, quantitative possessions and achievements to a new emphasis on less tangible, personal, qualitative capabilities and activities — from economic growth to personal and social growth.

In the economic sphere, maximum growth in the money value of society's activities, regardless of what they are, will no longer be the guiding principle. But that does not mean that growth in itself will become a dirty word. Growing will take place in other spheres. The industrial revolution has amplified our physical and intellectual capacities; our ability to care for our physical needs, to manufacture, to build, to travel, to transport, to communicate, to calculate, has grown enormously. The post-industrial revolution will amplify our psychological and social capabilities; our ability to develop ourselves, to understand one another, to support one another, to share in the life of the cosmos — that is what will grow.

Nor does the shift to sufficiency rather than growth as the guiding principle of economic life mean that all economic growth should cease. Millions of people in the world are still materially deprived; a top priority will be to enable them to meet their basic economic needs; and that will require more purposeful economic development than in the past. For most young adults there will continue to be a time when personal economic growth is appropriate. One aspect of growing up, of becoming independent from parents, is economic; and when young adults start a family of their own, their need for housing space and domestic equipment inevitably grows. When we speak of a shift of emphasis away from economic growth, it does not mean we forget these things or ignore them.

The shift to sufficiency rather than growth as the guiding principle of economic life will, however, mean a big difference in the way people think about economic growth and set about achieving it. In recent years, rapid growth, steady growth, low growth, no growth, negative growth, a particular percentage (e.g. 6%) growth, organic growth, differential growth, healthy growth, and good growth have all had their advocates. In the SHE future we shall recognise that all these generalisations are unsound.

Economic activity is like other spheres of life: we want some things to grow, but not others. When good things grow the growth is healthy, and when bad things grow the growth is unhealthy or cancerous. Good gardening is not judged in terms of maximum, percentage or zero growth of aggregate vegetation. Good health is not judged in terms of maximum, percentage, or zero body growth aggregated over every organ and limb of a growing child. There are few important spheres of life in which reasonable people argue whether rapid, steady, low, zero, or even negative aggregate growth is the right objective to pursue for its own sake. Even statements that economic growth should be organic, differential, healthy or good will be seen to have little practical significance unless we define what specific goals and tasks they imply. And for our society to aim to increase GNP for its own sake will be regarded as just as absurd as for people to aim at continually rising levels of money income and expenditure, regardless of what satisfaction they get from earning an income and what satisfaction they get from spending it.

In a chapter called 'Ideas on the Move' in his book 'The Human Quality'[71] Aurelio Peccei, the founder of the Club of Rome, includes a discussion of growth. He describes what is happening as follows. 'We have thus moved from gross growth to self-reliant growth and sustainable growth, and then to organic growth and dynamic equilibrium. This is tantamount to rediscovering the obvious, of which we had all lost sight in our frenzied scramble towards growth at any cost — namely that good resides in equilibrium. While these ideas are entering the common domain, another advance is being made by the recognition that there is yet another and fundamental dimension of equilibrium — within man himself. After having satisfied certain minimal requirements of life and attained physical well-being, he develops a wide range of other needs, wants and yearnings about his security, comfort, beliefs, self-fulfilment, social position, and what is generally called quality of life. Development is the word generally used to embrace the reasonable satisfaction of all such human demands, and the concept of development is rapidly superseding that of growth.' Now, Peccei continues, a further change is needed, 'a reversal of the present concept of development, bringing it to focus not on the demand side of the human being but on his capacity to contribute, hence on his quality and creativity ... It is wrong and misleading to consider human requirements as the starting point of a new phase of human evolution. *Development of human quality and capacity alone can be the foundation of any further achievement* ... This is the direction towards which we should apply all our energies if we want really "to grow".'

As the prevailing paradigm of growth continues to shift, we shall no doubt seek insights from patterns of growth in plant and animal life. For example, as the new shoots and twigs of a tree take over the process of growth from the old wood, growth ceases in the trunk and main branches. Are the over-developed industrial countries like trees in which the old wood of economic activity is hardening and reaching the limits of its growth, while the buds of psychological and social development are forming the new shoots of growth? If the tree were a rose tree or a fruit tree, we would prune it — to get new growth in the right places. Is there an equivalent way of pruning old growth in the social and human sphere? All plants and creatures have a natural life cycle — birth, growth, maturity, decline and death. Do we forget this in our attempts to prolong life, not only for individual people but also for organisations and institutions? Finally, the existence of each plant or creature to some extent enables and to some extent prevents the growth of others; and by its eventual death, it may create conditions in which others can grow. Do we tend to forget that, as individuals and as part of the institutions to which we belong, we can create conditions for others to grow in, not only by growing ourselves but also by declining? Is this what Christians mean when they say Christ died that we may live? These are some of the questions raised by the shift to a new, more ecological paradigm of growth.

Work

The prevailing paradigm of work today conforms to the prevailing emphasis on institutionalised economic activity. The prevailing paradigm of work in the SHE future will reflect the shift of emphasis to de-institutionalised activity, and to social and psychological as opposed to economic growth. This new paradigm of work, like the new paradigms of power and wealth, will see work as something which individuals and groups of people define and create for themselves, not as something which is provided for them or which they demand as the dependents of employing institutions. The shift to the new paradigm of work will be one aspect of the transformation of society, from a state in which people are encouraged to be dependent on society's institutions for all the important aspects of their lives, to a state in which people are encouraged to take control for themselves.

We start with a brief description of the present paradigm of work. We note that, as the limits close in on conventional economic growth, this paradigm is already beginning to break down. We then look briefly at what the hyper-expansionist (HE) scenario would imply for the idea of work, and we examine the possibility that work in itself will become much less important. We reject that possibility in favour of a new, but equally important, paradigm of work: which we then describe. We conclude by considering a number of existing developments which could form a bridge between the old paradigm of work and the new, and which can be seen as potential steps in the

74

transition between the industrial past and the post-industrial future.

The most important aspect of the existing paradigm is the extent to which people identify with their job. 'With the coming of the industrial revolution it was no longer enough that a man should occupy his station and give glory to God — in the world in which most of us grew up and for a number of generations prior to that time it was more essential that a man be encouraged to hold a job for which he was being paid. What are you going to be? did not refer to a child's future characteristics as a person, but to his choice of occupation.'[72] The puritan work ethic is still very much alive, in the sense that people lose status in their own eyes and in others' if they cannot get a job. Moreover, the overdeveloped industrialised societies reify the concept of work: work is a job; it is done for an employer for pay; it counts in the employment statistics. Unpaid work does not count. Unemployed people are assumed to do no work. Even self-employed people suffer discrimination. National economic policies are drawn up in consultation with representatives of employers and employees, not with representatives of self-employed workers, unpaid workers and the unemployed.

As we saw in Chapter 2, however, the institutionalised economies are now reaching limits to the number of jobs, the amount of money, the quantity of goods, the standard of services, and the level of satisfaction they can provide. These limits are creating contradictions about work, which cannot be resolved within the existing paradigm.

First, work (in the form of jobs) is not available for many people who want it. This problem cannot now be solved by any approach which confines itself to the workings of the formal economy. From now on, in the developed economies of Europe, North America and Japan, there is no way that full employment of the conventional kind can be brought back. Competition with other developed countries and with industrialising countries in the third world, will require a continual improvement in productivity in the manufacturing and exportable services sectors. Automation and the microprocessor will intensify the effects of those competitive pressures and also wipe out many jobs in services like banking and in office work of all kinds. Think of the economy as being divided into four main sectors: a capital-intensive production sector (e.g. chemicals, automobiles); a large-scale services sector (e.g. universities, schools, hospitals, banks); a small-scale local sector; and the household/neighbourhood sector. It is clear that the first two offer declining prospects for employment from now on. This means that many more people than today will be active in the local and household sectors, in which much of the work does not take the form of regular jobs — and is, in other words, part of the informal economy.

Second, the nature of much of the work available in the form of jobs discourages people from doing it well. It is pointless and boring, if not worse, and it is alienating in the sense that it is being done for someone else — often an impersonal organisation. People no longer feel compelled to work hard at jobs which they dislike or which fail to engage their interest. The work ethic, at least in the sense of taking pride in one's work and wanting to do it well, cannot survive the increasingly widespread introduction of the kind of work which the development of an institutionalised economy involves. A new sort of work ethic may be beginning to emerge, reflecting a more discriminating attitude about how people are prepared to spend their working lives. So far as formal employment is concerned, trade unionists like Mike Cooley[48] have begun to campaign not just for the traditional right to work, but for the right to work on socially useful products. Others [73] have begun to campaign for people's right to enjoy the leisure forced on them by unemployment. Meanwhile, increasing numbers of men are coming to think that real life takes place in and around the home and local community rather than the factory and the office, and want to play a larger part in the work of the informal economy which takes place there.

Third, while the institutionalised economy fails to create enough work in the form of jobs and compels many people to do unsatisfying and pointless work in the form of jobs, much important work is not carried out at all. This includes especially the kind of work which would improve the quality of life — the creation of better surroundings and amenities, and the provision of personal care and attention to people. Work in the form of jobs is incapable of doing work that needs to be done.

The hyper-expansionist (HE) scenario for the future claims to offer a solution to the problem of work: as super-technology and almost universal automation make more and more existing work unnecessary, most people's leisure will increase; the working day, the working week, the working year, and the working life will all be reduced; most people will find their main satisfactions not in work but in leisure; the work ethic will more or less disappear. But this solution has a fatal flaw. The work ethic would not disappear for Daniel Bell's pre-eminent professional and technical class who would be responsible for the high technology and sophisticated theoretical knowledge upon

76

which that kind of post-industrial society would depend. Their work would be of vital importance. So that kind of society would suffer from a deep schizophrenia about work. The hoi polloi would have to be persuaded that work is unimportant, unsatisfying, unfulfilling, unnecessary; while the elites and their potential recruits would have to be continually impressed with the value of work and the high status which it confers. It just doesn't add up.

However, leaving aside the HE scenario, it is worth looking a little more closely at the possibility that the work ethic may be on the way out. Gurth Higgin discusses this possibility. As we saw in Chapter 1, his thesis[32] is that our society's traditional social project (that of overcoming scarcity) is withering; and that its leading social part (manufacturing industry) and its leading psychological part (an alienating willingness to dedicate one's life to being merely an instrument of work) are withering along with it. He argues as follows:

'Work in the service of the production of wealth is the leading part in our traditional system, and within the life space of the individual his work activity is likewise the leading part. Any approach towards improving the quality of life that is based on the assumptions of the old paradigm with economic man as its datum, whether such thinking takes the bourgeois or Marxist form, will take work as its leading part. If we are in the process of developing a new social project as a more relevant paradigm, then it will be for some part of their experience other than work that people will be searching as a new leading part in their lives. No aspect of life other than work has yet become sufficiently clarified to attract the social and psychological energy of a new leading part. Nevertheless, in spite of this lack of a new focus the pull of interest and energy away from the centrality of work in our lives is a fact. For many people, the idea of improving the quality of their work lives, although not unattractive, does not seem to be of central relevance to their current experience. They are more concerned to find a new and more satisfying focus for their lives than in reinforcing the declining old. In short, the quality of life is not divisible. If it considers only work, if it does not cover the total life space, for many it loses its relevance.'

Thus Higgin seems to suggest that work as such is on the way out. I do not contest that a change of the kind he discusses is taking place; but I interpret it differently. I see it as a shift of the prevailing paradigm of work, not as a rejection of work altogether. I believe that the old paradigm of work is losing credibility, and a new paradigm has

77

begun to emerge. A certain kind of work, dominant during the industrial age, is on the way out. A new kind, appropriate to a new age, is on the way in.

You can look at it like this. If most people ceased to care about work and concentrated on leisure, what would they do with their greatly increased leisure? If their leisure activities were of the kind which costs money, increasing leisure would increase their spending. But they won't be able to earn the extra money by doing more work. So how will they get it? Who will decide how much money everyone should get to support their leisure activities? On the other hand, if their leisure is of the kind that doesn't cost money, what will people be doing with it? If they are simply wasting time, they will get bored. On the other hand, if they are entertaining one another, looking after children and sick people, doing DIY activities in the garden or house or workshop, educating themselves, writing, playing music, and a whole range of other activities which are purposeful and satisfying, as well as being enjoyable, won't they think of some of these activities as work? The more fortunate amongst us already do work of that kind today.

As David Elliott[74] has pointed out, changes in our values and norms and attitudes to work and non-work could change the nature of work. Today 'such activities, tasks and responsibilities as housework, child-rearing, voluntary social work and artistic creation, while being vital to the maintenance and health of society, are not perceived or rewarded as work.' But that need not always be the case. In fact the prevailing concepts of work are already changing.

'Changing concepts of work, whether at the personal or at the community or social level or both, are inescapably related to a changing sense of purpose — of what it is useful to do ... the labour market cannot much longer elicit credibility as an organising device for the activity of working or distributing income ... the concept of work as something that must be socially productive in the eyes of the beholder is coming to be used to sort meaningful from empty jobs. ... A whole new concept of work is emerging which will dismiss as work much which now passes for it and will embrace as work much which is not now included in it. ... Local Initiative Programs and similar schemes, designed out of a labour market mentality which was concerned to "create jobs," have served another and much more important purpose, the redefining of work for some of those who were ready to move in this direction. ... We are going to need to rely increasingly on individuals and communities to define their own concepts of work. . . . The enormous intellectual and social ferment of our times (whether we label it as future shock, or the transition to post-industrial society, the emergence of Consciousness III or the stable state, or childhood's end) is the context for changing concepts of work.'[72]

So what can we say about the new paradigm of work which is, I suggest, already beginning to emerge?

The dominant paradigm of work in Western Europe and North America in the 19th and 20th centuries emerged from the individualist, puritan ethic which was generated by the Reformation and confirmed by the industrial revolution. As that period of history comes towards an end, will we go back to pre-industrial or pre-Reformation paradigms of work? I do not think so, at least not exactly. The traditional Roman Catholic doctrine that bodily labour was decreed by Providence for the good of man's body and soul has a too authoritarian smack; it leaves the door too wide open to feudal exploitation of the work of the poor and the weak by the rich and powerful. The new work ethic may certainly have something in common with the work ethic of the Benedictine monasteries: 'Labour was to be man's greatest joy and the instrument of his union with God. Industry was the key to the upbuilding of the new world that Benedict created within the precincts of his monastic establishment. Everything was seen as an aspect of work. The singing of the divine office in church was the *opus Dei,* the work of prayer to God that is peculiar to the monk. It had to be done well. Manual labour was in its way, however, no less important in the life of the monastery, which could only exist through the support of the monk's hands. . . . Christ had redeemed human toil, making the humblest chore a labour of love. The dignity of labour was proved in the joy of a good monk's life. Work was but the highest expression of love.'[58] But even there, the notion of work as something that had to be redeemed by Christ appears to detract from the idea that work itself should be one of the main sources of human joy and satisfaction.

The new paradigm of work will, I believe, owe quite a lot to what Schumacher[42] has called Buddhist economics. He says that the Buddhist point of view takes the function of work to be threefold: to give a man a chance to utilise and develop his faculties; to enable him to overcome his ego-centredness by joining with other people in a common task; and to bring forth the goods and services needed for a becoming existence. This is not unlike William Morris's view that 'a man at work, making something which he feels will exist because he is working at it and wills it, is exercising the energies of his mind and soul as well as of his body. . . . If we work thus we will be men, and our days will be happy and eventful.'[75] But I believe that both Schumacher and William Morris underestimated the significance of increasing economic equality between men and women, the changing value and status that we give to what the industrial age has thought of as men's work and women's work, and therefore also the centrally important change that will probably take place in our relative valuation of paid and unpaid work.

I suggest that the new paradigm of work which is now emerging will see work as something which every human being should be able to take satisfaction in doing. Work, whether paid or unpaid, will signify those activities which are undertaken to satisfy human needs — one's own and other people's; and those needs will be assumed to include the higher level needs for love, esteem and personal growth as well as the basic needs for food, clothing, shelter and safety. Work will no longer be regarded as a chore — as something to be endured by the less fortunate (like the slaves in ancient Greece), to be shirked whenever possible, and ultimately to be abolished by automation. It will no longer be regarded as a job, to be created and preserved, counted and recorded, for its own sake. In a sane, humane, ecological society work will be necessary and desirable activity which confirms people in the knowledge of their own worth, which confirms the meaning of their relationships with other people, and which confirms their unity with the natural environment in which they live.

So by what transitional steps will the shift come about from the industrial to the post-industrial paradigm of work?[76] It will happen as measures taken to deal with today's problems of unemployment provide stepping stones to new patterns of work for the future. It will happen as the breakdown of full employment in the formal economy pushes people into work in the informal economy. It will happen as the attraction of the more personal way of working in the informal economy, and the growing perception that this is where real life takes place, draws people — especially men — away from pointless, impersonal activity in factories and offices. The problems of the formal economy and the opportunities of the informal economy will interact on one another. New patterns of actual work will interact with new perceptions of what good work should be about.

Response to the shortages of work in the formal economy will increasingly include: ways of sharing the available employment more widely; ways of providing special opportunities for employment to particular categories of people, e.g. young people; ways of providing opportunities for employment on certain categories of project not normally undertaken by the formal economy, e.g. community enterprises; and ways of easing the entry into informal work, e.g. voluntary work, of people who are made redundant or who retire early.

There is a wide variety of ways of sharing employment more widely. They involve shortening the working day, the working week, the working year, and the working life of the individual worker. They include part-time work, job-sharing, longer holidays, sabbaticals, early retirement, and a postponement — for example, by longer education and training or by a period of community service — of the entry of young people into the job market. All these approaches, except the last, result in people having a greater proportion of their time to spend working in the informal economy. All, except the last, encounter two main problems: people are reluctant to accept shorter time in employment if this means a proportionate reduction in their pay; and there is pressure on women to accept that the more flexible part-time patterns of work opened up by these approaches are more suitable for them than they are for men. Both these problems will become less severe as and when the link between paid work and money income is further loosened, and the attractions of having more time to spend on informal work become valued more highly — by men as well as women.

The provision of special employment opportunities on special types of project, though it has so far been aimed at easing the situation created by the shortage of formal employment, is also helping to open up new areas of work in the small-scale, local community sector. That, as we have seen, will be one of the growth sectors for work in the post-industrial economy, and much of the work in it is somewhat informal in character. These measures, like the various job-sharing approaches discussed in the previous paragraph, can thus help to provide stepping-stones to new post-industrial patterns of work for the future.

Many employers and personnel managers have now begun to introduce schemes for early redundancy and retirement, for helping middle-aged employees to re-orientate their lives and to find alternative fields of work — including voluntary work — to suit their preferences, for helping former employees to set up businesses of their own, and to switch existing employees from full-time to part-time employment. All these initiatives too, while being primarily aimed at resolving employment problems of the formal economy, are helping to provide stepping stones to a new pattern of work in which informal and voluntary work will be much more important than they have been.

However, the top-down approach to the problems of unemployment in the formal economy can never be successful on its own. Its central weakness is its assumption that provision of occupation for the unfortunate unemployed is a task for the fortunate employed. Only when the top-down approach becomes subordinate and complementary to the bottom-up approach of increasing numbers of self-motivated people trying to create valuable occupations for themselves, will the attempt to promote job-sharing, part-time employment, small businesses, co-operatives, community enterprises, and so on, take off in a really successful way. Revival of the informal economy in which people work for themselves and one another on tasks which are valuable to themselves, will be an essential stimulus to the successful decentralisation, slimming down and modernisation of the formal economy.

This leads us to the fundamental realities of employment and work which our societies are beginning to confront. These realities can be summarised as follows.

The industrial age has been the only period of human history in which most people's work has taken the form of jobs. The industrial age is now coming to an end, and many of the changes in work patterns which it brought will have to be reversed. To the conventional mind this seems a daunting thought. But, in fact, it could offer the prospect of a better future for work. Universal employment, as its history shows, has not meant economic freedom.

Employment became widespread when the enclosures of the 17th and 18th centuries made many people dependent on paid work, by depriving them of the use of land and thus of the means to provide a living for themselves. Then the factory system destroyed the cottage industries and removed work from people's homes. Later, as transport improved, first by rail and then by road, people commuted longer distances to their places of employment until, eventually, many people's work lost all connection with their home lives and the places in which they lived.

Meanwhile, employment put women at a disadvantage. In pre-industrial times, men and women had shared the productive work of the household and village community. Now it became customary for the husband to go out to paid employment, leaving the unpaid work of the home and family to his wife. Tax and benefit regulations still assume this norm today, and restrict more flexible sharing of work roles between the sexes. And it was not only women whose work status suffered. As employment became the dominant form of work, young people and old people were excluded — a problem now, as more teenagers become frustrated at school and more retired people want to live active lives.

In modern times, public policy has assumed that work means employment. The interests of employers and employees have been consulted by governments. No other workers, such as housewives or the self-employed, have enjoyed the same privilege. Public money, including depreciation allowances and tax reliefs as well as outright grants, has been given to firms and other employing organisations on the assumption that they and they only are capable of organising people's work. Nobody has thought of redistributing some of the nation's capital to people, rather than organisations, and giving people the wherewithal to work for themselves.

All this will now have to change. The time has come to switch effort and resources away from the obsolete goal of creating jobs for all, to the urgent practical tasks of helping many people to manage without full-time jobs and of easing the transition to a new work order.

More and more people are clearly going to need a source of basic income other than wage or salary. They will also have to be allowed and helped:

— to top up this basic income with irregular paid work or regular part-time employment;

— to supplement their money income by productive 'leisure' activities such as food-growing and all kinds of DIY (do-it-yourself activities), thus providing some goods and services for themselves instead of buying them;[77]

— to acquire facilities of their own (including land, buildings, workshops and equipment) to enable them to work on their own account or as members of family and neighbourhood groups;

— to build up 'sweat equity', for example by building their homes themselves instead of working as employees to pay off a mortgage;

— to learn the skills to do these things, instead of much of the job-oriented education and training which people are offered today.[78]

A top priority will be to change the existing system of taxes and benefits. First, all citizens, male and female, should be treated equally, as individuals, without discrimination. Next, we must stop discouraging people from useful activity if they are not employed. The neatest solution will be a guaranteed basic income for everybody, perhaps in the form of a negative income tax.[79] Finally, depreciation allowances and other investment incentives should be given for productive equipment installed in people's homes, as well as in factories and offices belonging to companies.

Planning regulations will also have to be changed. They assume that most people will work on employers' premises. They often prevent people working in or near their homes. More broadly, we must rethink what development means. Development agencies now concentrate on attracting employers to an area — usually from somewhere else! In future they should find ways of helping local people to support themselves.

One important factor, technology, points in the right direction. Advanced, inexpensive equipment and materials are becoming available for small-scale productive work in many fields: food-growing and food-processing; energy conservation and supply; carpentry, plumbing, electrics and other aspects of building construction and maintenance; textiles and clothing; and, of course, information technology. Whereas the new technology of 200 years ago drove production out of the home and neighbourhood into the factory and the town, the new technology of today will bring much of it back again.

The main problem, and the main obstacle to the shift to a new paradigm of work, is political. Most leading people in business, trade unions and the public services, in management and the professions, together with politicians and economists of all persuasions, are deeply committed to employment as the way of work. The idea of a wider range of options, that would liberate millions of people from the alternatives of depending either on an employer for a job or on the state for the dole, is hard for them to swallow.

In Britain in the early 19th century, the Whigs and Tories for a long time refused to accept that an industrial society had replaced the old agricultural society. By delaying repeal of the Corn Laws[80] and putting off the introduction of cheap food, they caused unnecessary hardship and distress to many working people. All the industrial countries are facing an equally profound transition now — from an age of universal employment to a new work order. By refusing to recognise this and to ease the transition to a new paradigm of work, the various branches of today's establishment in these countries are imposing unnecessary hardship and distress on many millions of jobless people.

A society which continues to condition its members to believe that they should all have a job, but is incapable of providing jobs for them, is inflicting grave damage on them and on itself. This situation must be brought to an end as soon as possible, and the only way this can happen is by a shift to a new paradigm of work. As the example of work clearly shows, the paradigm shift is no mere question of abstract theorising, of interest only to intellectuals. It is a matter of grave, practical urgency from a common-sense, humanitarian point of view.

Metaphysical Reconstruction

Our concern in this chapter has been with those ideas, or paradigms, which shape our outlook and our way of life and are embodied in our institutions. We have discussed shifts in the prevailing paradigms of wealth, power, growth and work. As we move into the SHE future, comparable paradigm shifts will occur in every other sphere.

In each case these paradigm shifts will be facets of a larger, more fundamental shift in our prevailing world view. The shift from the mediaeval to the modern era was accompanied by a shift from a view of the world as hierarchically organised in subordination to God, to a view of the world as a machine which humans could understand and control from outside. The shift to the post-industrial era will be accompanied by a shift from that mechanistic, instrumental view of the world to a developmental view of a living world in which human consciousness and human action are experienced as integral with the processes and relationships with which they are concerned. This new world view will be one which reflects and confirms the personal, interpersonal and ecological values implied by the vision of a SHE future. It has been outlined by an increasing number of scientists and thinkers in recent years.[36]

Changes in ideas and changes in activity are related to one another as chickens are to eggs. Both come first; both come second. The transformation of society results in the transformation of its dominant ideas. For example, as the prevailing forms of political and economic activity change, the prevailing paradigms of power and wealth adapt. But, equally important, the transformation of dominant ideas results in the transformation of society. As thinkers and philosophers pursue their proper task of metaphysical reconstruction (Schumacher's phrase[42]) — as they work to bring into focus a coherent constellation of new ideas about wealth, power, growth, work, etc. — the prevailing outlook and the prevailing forms of activity in society will adapt to this new framework of perception. Thus the push of events changes our thinking, and the pull of our new thinking changes the course of events.

Among the strongest reasons for doubting whether mankind will avoid catastrophe in the next 30 or 40 years is the power of vested interests and the interlocked inertia of institutions. For myself, 20 years' experience of big government, big business and big finance convinced me that people in positions of so-called power within that system have comparatively little power of constructive action. They are prisoners of a blocked system, trapped in an interacting complex of escalating pressures and confrontations of the kind which Gregory Bateson[81] called schismogenic. The institutional imperative restricts the choice of acceptable solutions to those that will make the problems worse.

However, as Keynes said, 'the power of vested interests is vastly exaggerated, compared with the gradual encroachment of ideas.' The encroachment of ideas that we have been discussing here will eventually loosen the blockages in the existing institutional system. It must be purposefully pursued. The practical need is for more awareness — including more thinking, discussion and writing — about the emergence of these new paradigms and their role in society's transformation. In a sane, humane, ecological society what will most people understand by knowledge, learning, justice, teaching, welfare, caring, health, healing, growth, work, power, public service, and so on? What will be the practical consequences, as these concepts lose their present meanings and take on new ones? In aggregate, what new prevailing ideology or metaphysic will eventually be created for a new society by these conceptual changes? In the next few years these questions will continue be the subject of a growing spate of books, pamphlets, tracts, lectures, seminars, conferences and group discussions.

5
A Process of Transformation

Moving into the SHE future will involve a change of direction in the development of modern societies — a transformation of society and of ourselves. This process will be immensely complex. It will be accomplished more smoothly if we understand its nature. So in this chapter we consider what kind of a direction change this will be, and we discuss various aspects of the transformation process. We thus prepare the ground for the discussion of practical action in the final chapter.

Upward Spiral

What kind of a direction change should we envisage, then, as we turn towards the SHE future? I suggest that we think of the five competing scenarios in the following way.

A Business-As-Usual future would imply that we continue to proceed in the same general direction as hitherto, and a little upwards; unspectacular progress would continue. The Disaster scenario would imply that we plummet downwards, losing much of the ground we have gained in the past. The AC future would imply that we freeze things and stay where we are: Stop! The HE future would imply a deliberate acceleration of dominant recent trends, in a marked upward and forward movement. The SHE scenario can best be understood as an upward spiral, in the sense that we shall move upward to better things while also, in certain respects, doubling back on the past. For example, we shall put great emphasis on self-help as was done by Samuel Smiles and others in the 19th century; but we shall not leave people to go to the wall if they fail; we shall enable them to help themselves. Again, more work will come back into the home and the local community; but on a democratic basis, without returning to patriarchal domination in the home or squirearchical domination in the local community. Yet again, more of us will live more self-sufficient lives on our own piece of land than in modern industrial society; but advanced small-scale technology will enable us to live much better than our pre-industrial ancestors did. The idea of an

87

upward spiral has many applications of this kind.

Breakdown/Breakthrough

The coming transformation can also be understood as a process of breakdown and breakthrough — breakdown of the old and breakthrough to the new.

Powerful trends are combining to create a breakdown in existing values, existing lifestyles and existing institutions. These trends include: domination by big technology, exhaustion of natural resources, pollution, unemployment, inflation, a general paralysis of institutions, widespread personal helplessness, and so on. Meanwhile, new growth points are emerging which could converge to create a breakthrough to a new and better society. These new growth points include: a new emphasis on self-help, self-reliance and self-sufficiency; a new balance between the sexes; a growing interest in social, economic and political structures which serve people rather than dominate them; a growing commitment to appropriate technologies which do the same; a growing feeling that we are all inhabitants of the same planet, citizens of the same world; a growing ecological consciousness; and an increasing interest in a spiritual and cosmic approach to life, summarily described by the terms supernature and supermind.

Another way of looking at breakdown/breakthrough is closely relevant to the paradigm shifts discussed in Chapter 4. Overdeveloped institutional and intellectual structures can be seen as an important part of what is beginning to break down, and personal experience and action an important part of what should be encouraged to break through — as follows:

breakdown	*breakthrough*
scientific and academic knowledge	intuitive understanding
representative politics and bureaucratic government	community politics and direct democracy
the institutional economy based on money and jobs	the gift and barter economy of households and local communities
an arm's length relationship between professionals and their clients	personally shared experience

| institutionalised social services | caring personal relationships |
| organised religious activity and codified religious doctrines | personal spiritual experience |

The relationship between the first and second of each of these opposing pairs — as also the relationship between city and country, between industrialised and third world peoples, between men and women, and between the left and right sides of the brain — has become very asymmetrical in the modern industrialised world, to the point where the first has over-shadowed and threatened to suppress the second. As the well-known religious thinker Raimundo Panikkar put it in a somewhat different context, 'Applying *logos* to the myth, amounts to killing the myth: it is like looking for darkness with a torch.'[82] Applying laboratory tests to spiritual healing, or bureaucratic scrutiny to community self-help, or cost-benefit analysis to social innovation, destroys the conditions in which spiritual healing, community self-help or social innovation can take place — like looking for darkness with a torch. But now these asymmetrical relationships are beginning to break down. In every case the same kind of questions are beginning to arise — about creativity and the upsurge of new aspirations. In every case a new relationship will have to be developed. It will be based on harmony and balance rather than on domination and subservience. It will be achieved by decolonising the old structures and liberating the new energies.

These concepts of decolonisation and liberation are crucial. If an old order is breaking down and we want a new one to break through, two principal tasks clearly present themselves. The first is to manage the breakdown of the old order in such a way as to avoid catastrophic collapse and untold hardship for the vast majority of people who depend upon it for almost every aspect of their lives. The second is to foster the growth points which will eventually provide the foundations on which a new society can be built. The first is a task of decolonisation; the second is a task of liberation. They are, of course, the two sides of a single coin.

Many thinkers about the transformation — or revolution — which we now face, concentrate on the second of these two sides only. Murray Bookchin's essays[30] on 'post-scarcity anarchism', 'ecology and revolutionary thought', 'liberatory technology' and 'forms of freedom' are good examples of the best thinking of the 1960s and early 1970s. They emphasise the centrality of liberation: 'The problems of social reconstruction have been reduced to practical tasks that can be solved spontaneously by self-liberatory acts of society ... A libertarian society can be achieved only by a libertarian revolution. Freedom cannot be delivered as an end-product of a revolution.' Now, of course it is perfectly true that people cannot be given power, they must take it for themselves and create it by their own learning in action — just as adolescents must do their own growing up. But at the same time it is a great mistake to forget the other side of the picture. Those who have power can learn to give it away before it crumbles — they can help other people to take it, just as enlightened parents can help their adolescent children to grow up.

Decolonisation

People who continue to work in the institutionalised and professionalised structures of society — as politicians, civil servants, businessmen, industrialists, bankers, scientists, teachers, doctors, planners, trade unionists, and so on — have a vital part to play in the coming transformation of society. But they must decide which side they are on. Are they working for some variant of a hyper-expansionist, elitist, institutionalised, authoritarian future — the AC or HE futures of Chapter 1 — in which people like themselves will dominate other people? Are they simply coasting along in their comparatively privileged position? Or are they ready to commit themselves to work for a sane, humane, ecological future? Do they recognise that, as Ivan Illich has said about scientific discoveries, their expertise can be used in two different ways, and are they prepared to choose the second? 'The first leads to specialisation of functions, institutionalisation of values and centralisation of power, and turns people into accessories of bureaucracies or machines; the second enlarges the range of each person's competence, control and initiative, limited only by other individuals' claims to an equal range of power and freedom.'[83] Are they prepared to use their skills, their experience and their position to enlarge the range of other people's autonomy? Are they prepared to give away their own relative superiority?

There are already signs of professional people trying to develop an enabling role rather than a dominating one. Some remarks made at a conference in Ottawa in 1974 on the future of the serving professions[84] will serve to illustrate the possibility of professionals helping their patients, customers and clients to become less dependent on them and to increase their self-reliance.

'The institutionalisation of service-providing bureaucracies turns the client into a consumer, creating yet another barrier between the professional and the real person.'

'Professionals should share rather than monopolise their privileged knowledge, give people a chance to learn while they are healing.'

'Until a conscious majority brings about economic and social changes to provide the basis for a truly human society, a sane society, we all can only do our best, wherever we are, to demystify, expose, act *with* people on problems, not *for* them.'

'The individual has little feeling for participation in our present society because of social structures in which the professions hold a major power base. Is radical social change possible, given the present state of professional institutions?'

'The professions are as subject to the "greatest crisis of our times", the personal identity crisis, as anyone else in contemporary urban society. Without their professional definition many would feel extremely threatened. Is is realistic, given the alientating nature of our cities, to expect people to give up these identities?'

'Professionals as a group have abdicated their responsibility in terms of effecting social change.'

'Are professionals prepared to give up middle class standards and prestige in order to get closer to those they serve?'

'Lawyers under the present system are paid antagonists hired to fight with one another on behalf of others who want expertise with non-involvement.'

'If poverty is basically the absence of power, social action must involve giving people part of this power back. We lawyers should be training people to understand the law and apply it to represent themselves.'

'This "Me God, you stupid" attitude of the doctor towards the patient, which stems from professional insecurity, is a kind of refined violence.'

'The question we must seriously ask ourselves is to what extent are we as physicians prepared to disappear? What we should be asking in our relationships with patients is "What have I done so this person can manage to do without me in the future?"'

'Among the social pitfalls fostered by the professions is the trend towards overdependency which verges on helplessness. Among the questions we professionals must ask ourselves is whether we are helpers or hinderers. Are we creating an endless production of services that draw us further into a trap? Do we, through the framing of laws and other structures create barriers that we then must spend valuable time breaking down again?'

Here are a few examples of the idea that managers and professional people should help people to help themselves, rather than monopolise their expertise so as to keep people dependent on them. The Association of Karen Horney Psycho-analytic Counsellors[85] was set up to aid untrained people to gain skills in psychoanalytic self-analysis, to build up a basic group of highly skilled counsellors and teachers, to introduce co-operative methods on as wide a scale as possible, and to train people working in neighbourhood, community, voluntary and health projects. In a completely different field, the Royal Bank of Canada has set up Community Branches, designed to provide banking services 'to people on welfare as well as to the working poor, in order to begin to build bridges from the culture of poverty into the mainstream of Canadian life. This includes counselling and referral services and provides meeting space in front of the branch for the people in the community so that they can teach themselves how to manage their funds, assess their financial problems, and derive workable solutions.'[86] John Turner and his colleagues in the architectural and planning professions are developing practical concepts of 'freedom to build' and 'housing by people', as opposed to the conventional assumption of most housing, building and planning agencies, and most of their professional and administrative agents, that any new or newly perceived housing problem must be perceived as a demand for a new programme.[87] Alice Coleman[88] has argued for an approach to environmental planning which will enlarge people's options rather than restrict them; for example, environments can be designed in which a large range of destinations — homes, shops, workplaces, schools, hospitals, and so on — are located within short distances of one another thus providing accessibility and giving people genuine options of walking or cycling.

This enabling ethic is applicable to every sphere of organised life, including business, government, trade unions, the public services, communications and the media, and entertainment. It would provide the underlying principle for the decolonisation of institutionalised society. It suggests that people who work in government, business, trade unions and finance, should act so as to reduce people's economic dependence on jobs, on money, and on goods and services provided by industry, commerce and the public services. It suggests that people who are trained and experienced journalists, broadcasters, managers and technicians in the press and broadcasting media, should help their existing and potential readers, listeners and viewers to become less dependent on them for their information and entertainment. In Chapter 6 we shall suggest a comprehensive basis for discussing the practical possibilities. But here are some examples for business and government.

Oil companies have seen their role in industrial society as selling increasing quantities of oil. In the SHE society, oil companies will aim to help their customers to buy less oil, by reducing their dependence on it. In other words, the nature of the oil business will change from producing and selling oil, to helping people to meet their energy needs. Similarly, pharmaceutical and food manufacturing firms have set out to sell increasing quantities of drugs and convenience foods. In the SHE society they will help their customers to reduce their dependence on these products. The nature of the business will then have changed from producing and selling health products and food products, to helping people to meet their health needs and food needs.

So far as governments are concerned, instead of continuing to build up capital-intensive industry, centralised energy systems, and bureaucratic public services, thereby increasing people's dependence upon them for work, for material needs and for social wellbeing — governments will shift the emphasis to policies which help people to become more self-sufficient and autonomous. For example:

they will support *decentralised* energy production and conservation;

they will develop *job creation programmes,* not so much as a centralised policy for providing more jobs, but in order to foster economic self-reliance at the local community level;

they will encourage the kind of *investment in housing and other local facilities* (including gardens, workshops, etc.) which will help to develop the economic and social self-reliance of households and local communities;

they will encourage *rural resettlement* and small-scale agriculture.

So far as management is concerned, a recent report on 'Management for the Twenty-First Century'[6] stated that 'many managers will probably have learned how to give managerial power away, how to enable former employees (or former parts of the corporation) to work independently, and how to develop new patterns of organised activity and work based on arrangements of contract and trust.' The same report suggested that managers may find that enabling other people (including groups and communities) to develop themselves provides them with a new guiding principle for their work.

Those then are the kinds of changes decolonisation will involve. Now for some of the problems.

For a start, there is the problem of domination and dependence. For many of the people in managerial, professional and governing positions, their personal identity and their lifetime's energy are invested in the importance of their present role and in the sense of other people's dependence on it. They will feel threatened by the possible loss of their existing position and their existing power, and they will cling to them neurotically. John Adams has said of the logical and mathematical models of society which so many social scientists try to use: 'Such models ... may represent for some shrunken souls the essence of society. But rather I suspect they represent a retreat from a reality that is too alarming to contemplate. They represent a proper Laingian case of schizophrenia, in which a real world that is frightening and obviously out of control is replaced by a more comforting fantasy world in which the planner is master'.[89] As the old system continues to break down, many managers, professionals, politicians, trade union leaders and other established leaders are likely to make increasingly authoritarian attempts to bolster the importance of the knowledge and skill, experience and power, which they have built up within it. At the same time, there will be many citizens, consumers, workers, patients and other clients of the existing structures who will cling to their dependence. They will feel threatened by the thought of having to take power and responsibility to themselves.

Some managerial and professional people will also have a genuinely altruistic reluctance to abdicate from responsiblity. Some people believe that the decolonising imperial powers abdicated their responsibilities in the 1950s and 1960s. Certainly there are places, such as Uganda, where decolonisation has been followed by a reversion to disorder, violence and tyranny. Many responsible people will genuinely fear that to decolonise the present institutions of industrialised society would be to abandon millions of people — who now depend on those institutions for physical, material and psychological security — to the tyranny of local rulers, the exploitation of local tycoons, the domination of local patriarchs, and the magic of local charlatans and witch doctors.

At the practical administrative level, routine practitioners will find it hard to justify 'enabling' policies according to the conventional criteria used by governments, business managements and the professions today. For example, suppose that a government decided to invest public money in a housing programme which would provide sufficient garden and workshop facilities to enable the occupants to become less dependent on money for buying food and household items, and less dependent on the labour market for work. Not only would the direct financial return on the investment be 'uneconomic' (according to conventional criteria about rates of return), but the investment would actually reduce the level of measured GNP. So, although a housing policy of this kind might be very successful and valuable in social and human terms, it would be unthinkable according to conventional criteria. No doubt there will be many examples in spheres such as education and health, where enabling policies will run counter to the conventional criteria used to evaluate new proposals today.

These difficulties and problems will be very real. They will not be solved theoretically in advance, but by the cumulative weight of new developments which show that in practice they must and can be overcome or ignored, and which thus erode their relevance. Abraham Maslow throws light on this aspect of transformation, on the process of transition from an old paradigm to a new one, when he speaks of tolerating 'the simultaneous existence and perception of inconsistencies, of oppositions, and of flat contraditions. These seem to be products of partial cognition, and fade away with cognition of the whole.'[90] Many people already recognise that the conventional criteria of profit and economic surplus are products of partial cognition.

Decolonisation was a historic task, a high endeavour, for many colonial administrators earlier this century. This was expressed as follows by the senior British official in one African territory writing confidentially to his colleagues in 1951 at a time of local crisis. 'One thing which is quite certain is that we are following the policy which is the British contribution to world political history . . . We need to recapture our mission, and to remember what we came to this country to do: to work for the wellbeing and the progress of the people . . . not to seek too much for ourselves, but to be the instruments of carrying out our country's policy loyally and tirelessly. And that policy is to lead these people onwards to govern themselves and eventually to decide for themselves what their future status as a country is to be . . . We have instilled democratic ideals into them; we have taught them to wish to govern themselves; the growth in political consciousness and in critical attitudes to the actions of government is what our own education and our own outlook on life and affairs have given them.'[91] The best among the British colonial adminstrators knew that they were working towards the achievement of their own redundancy. The roots of this policy went back many years to the Durham Report on Canada in 1837. Its culmination was marked by Harold Macmillan's 'wind of change' tour of Africa as Prime Minister in 1960. As we face the prospect of decolonising the overdeveloped institutions of industrialised society, we shall no doubt have something to learn from the successes and failures of Britain's and other European countries' colonial policies in the 19th and 20th centuries.

Liberation

If managing the breakdown of overdeveloped institutions can be seen as decolonisation, developing one's own and other people's self-reliance can be seen as liberation. In health, in education, at work, in housing, in food, in transport, in energy, in politics, in religion, and in other economic and social aspects of our lives, many of us need to liberate ourselves and others from excessive dependence — on money and jobs; on big organisations, big technology, and professionalised services; on cities; on men, if we are women, and on women if we are men; on the industrialised countries if we live in the third world; and on logic and the intellect, if our intuitions and emotions have been stunted and underdeveloped.

We can imagine this liberation movement as a post-industrial revolution, which parallels the industrial revolution in various important features. The industrial revolution, of course, was about technical and economic innovation and development whereas the post-industrial revolution will be about psychological and social innovation and development. This is the distinction to keep in mind, as we consider possible parallels with the industrial revolution that began in 18th century Britain — relying heavily for this purpose on Peter Mathias' 'The First Industrial Nation'.[92]

The first significant point is that the industrial revolution by-passed the established order. There was no question of conscious government policy sponsoring industrial progress. The industrial revolution occurred spontaneously, behind the back of the state and of the ruling classes of the time. We may expect the post-industrial revolution similarly to by-pass the established order today. If the dominant institutions of industrial society — government, industry, finance, trade unions, public services, universities and professions — are uninterested in promoting psychological and social innovation and growth, that is no cause for alarm.

Second, government in 18th century Britain was more permissive towards new economic activity than in other countries like France. Moreover, the social structure and social attitudes of 18th century Britain were more flexible than in any other European country, except perhaps for Holland. Increasing religious heterodoxy meant that various groups, particularly of Protestant non-conformists like Quakers, were developing their own social ethics and economic roles along with their own theology. Today, prevailing attitudes of permissiveness and flexibility towards social and psychological innovation are likely to provide fruitful conditions for the post-industrial revolution; and among today's (not religious, but secular) non-conforming groups we are likely to find its active pioneers.

Third, one of the main pre-requisites for the industrial revolution was the existence of economic resources sufficient in quantity and conveniently positioned to develop new dimensions to the economy. In 18th century Britain plentiful coal and iron ore were conveniently placed for water transport in many parts of the country, and a strategic river system, based on the rivers Trent and Severn, stretched into the heart of industrial England. A corresponding pre-requisite for the post-industrial revolution will clearly be the existence of social resources sufficient in strength and so related to one another that from them can be developed new dimensions to society. These social resources could include: large numbers of active people leisured or unemployed; large numbers of active people educated and socially aware; the existence of education, information and communication systems which are not altogether closed to new ideas, not altogether dominated by economic, social and political forces committed to the status quo; and a widespread awareness that psychological and social development has become as important, if not more important, than economic and commercial development.

Another factor in the industrial revolution was inventiveness, a readiness to use other people's ideas and skills, and the capacity to generate an increasing flow of technical innovations through which physical production and productivity could be increased. The post-industrial revolution will also need inventiveness — to generate an increasing flow of social innovations, through which the psychological and social counterparts to physical production and productivity can be increased. These will be to do with teaching, learning and the sharing of new consciousness.

97

Again, a new breed of entrepreneurs played a special part in the energetic experimentation and technical innovation which marked the industrial revolution. These were the men, Mathias says, 'under whose charge new sectors of the economy could be developed and inventions brought into productive use. Such men were the shock troops of economic change.' In the post-industrial revolution entrepreneurs of social change will play a comparable role, facilitating new types of social and psychological growth and helping to bring social and psychological innovations into widespread use.

Innovation in industry in 18th century Britain also required the investment of financial capital in the productive process. New channels had to be created, through which savings could flow to the people who wanted to use them from the people who had spare money to invest. In due course there developed a linked national network of financial institutions, including the country banks, and the bankers, billbrokers and other specialist intermediaries in the City of London, to handle the transfer of credit from one part of the country to another; and the habit of productive financial investment became established. What will be the post-industrial counterparts to financial capital, to the banking networks, and to the habit of productive financial investment? Instead of money, shall we be concerned with psychological and social energy? Will there be people with surplus psychological and social energy to invest in other people's projects, in the confident expectation of receiving psychological and social — rather than commercial — reward from their investment? What sort of people are these, what is the nature of their support for the social entrepreneur, what reward do they seek, how shall we identify them, and how shall we create the channels to link them with the social entrepreneurs and social innovators who need their backing? Will inter-personal networks of volunteers provide such channels? Will activist minorities, linked with one another and receiving support through these networks, disseminate the psychological and social changes of the post-industrial revolution?[93]

To sum up, the industrial revolution was a self-sustaining cumulative process of industrial innovation centred upon what Mathias calls the 'new matrix of industries, materials and skills', in which steam power, coal, iron machinery, and engineering skills played the dominant part. This new matrix gave increasing freedom from the limitations of the physical capabilities of human beings which had held back economic activity in all previous ages. We should expect the post-industrial revolution similarly to become a self-sustaining process, in which a new matrix of psycho-social resources, techniques and skills (corresponding to Mathias' matrix of industries, materials and engineering skills) will give increasing freedom from the limitations of personal and institutional capabilities which have held back psychological and social growth hitherto.

Imagining the new liberation movement in this way, participating in its specific activities, and understanding and communicating its progress as it develops, will all be important ways of helping it to come about. Realism will be needed. Many new endeavours will fail, though they make a positive contribution nonetheless. People will only support a new initiative if it offers something they want and seems likely to be a better use of their time and energy than other ways of spending them. Although the main objective of these endeavours will not be technological achievement or financial profit, they will fail if they are technically incompetent or financially irresponsible. Many charlatans, tricksters, cranks, free riders and born losers will join this bandwagon, as they have done with every other new movement in history, and it will often be difficult to distinguish them from genuine pioneers. Effective partners in this new social revolution will need good judgement and staying power as well as enthusiasm and new age values.

Psychology of Transformation

The idea of a breakdown of an old way of life and a breakthrough to a new one suggests parallels with the decline of the old and the growth of the new in nature's cycles: death and birth; evening and morning; winter and spring. It may also remind us of situations in our personal lives, when the end of one phase and the beginning of another is accompanied by regret for what is over, grief for past failure, hope for the future, expectation of things to come. Some people see it as a parallel with religious ideas and resurrection, and think of the 'evolutionary leap into the new age made by the Son of Man'.[94]

It is possible to view the present crisis of mankind as a crisis of adolescence, a time of change from dependence and irresponsibility to independence and responsibility. The SHE future requires the internalisation of social control (for example in worker managed or socially responsible business enterprises) and the development of personal and group self-reliance. The SHE future can thus be seen to depend on society's development from childhood to adulthood, whereas the regulations and controls of an authoritarian society imply that childhood continues. The relationship between decolonisers and liberators can be undestood as a relationship between parents and growing up children.

On the other hand, Stephen Verney[94] argues that the challenge before us is to grow from independence to interdependence. He says, 'It is commonly suggested that mankind is now coming of age, which is taken to mean, by those who use the phrase, that we are arriving at mature wisdom. But a boy or girl comes of age at eighteen, and this is not the time of mature wisdom but the end of adolescence. It is the stage when he or she is emerging from a rebellion against parental authority and preparing for marriage, and for making a responsible contribution to society. If the Renaissance can be understood as a period when we in Europe broke out of a hierarchical order into an age of individualism — if at least the emphasis of that collective change was from dependence to independence — then we might understand our own generation as a time when the emphasis must be on interdependence — we must stop behaving like irresponsible adolescent individualists.'

Or perhaps we are going through a mid-life crisis. Gurth Higgin[95] describes this as a centroversion crisis, and explains as follows: 'The individual dominated by an active thrusting ego goes through the first half of life establishing a job and a family and settling an adult identity. ... He has little trouble from his internal world. This is damped down and contained. ... But then comes what is usually called the mid-life crisis. ... It is precipitated by a lessening of ego activity. ... The individual comes to realise that his life, job or career pattern is settled. ... The ego slows down a little, softens its outward thrust. The whole system relaxes and reflects. ... All the wondering questions about identity, about the value for himself of what he does with his life, about what he believes in, plague his mind. ... There is only finite time — is he doing what he really wants to do, is he really the person he really wants to be?' Peter Draper,[40] a doctor, takes a similar view in his advice to the British economy: 'You seem to be going through a kind of middle-age crisis, you are on the edge of a new phase of life, what some social physicians have called a "post-industrial" state. Try to sort out what it is you want to accomplish; talk about it, so that appropriate courses of action will make themselves more apparent. And don't, please, go on holiday with any of the other hypochondriacs in your neighbourhood. If you need company, choose friends who can concentrate on goals and values. You have the age and experience to sort things out — and only you can decide what you want to make of your life.'

Willis Harman[12] has drawn attention to the fact that breakdown/breakthrough is a component in the transformation both of individuals and of societies. He says, 'All we have learned of psychotherapy suggests that it is at the precise time when the individual feels as if his whole life is crashing down around him that he is most likely to achieve an inner reorganisation constituting a quantum leap in his growth towards maturity. Our hope, our belief, is that it is precisely when society's future seems so beleaguered — when its problems seem almost staggering in complexity, when so many individuals seem alienated, and so many values seem to have deteriorated — that it is most likely to achieve a metamorphosis in society's growth toward maturity, toward more truly enhancing and fulfilling the human spirit than ever before. Thus we envision the possibility of an evolutionary leap to a trans-industrial society that not only has know how, but also has a deep inner knowledge of what is worth doing.'

The coming transformation of society will be accomplished more effectively and peacefully if we understand the practical psychology of it. For example, it is not hard to guess that dominant and dependent character types will resist decolonisation and liberation, since their sense of security rests on domination or dependence; and it is fairly obvious that most people whose livelihood, welfare and identity depend on business or finance, politics or government, the public services or the trade unions, will feel threatened by the new paradigms of wealth, power, growth and work discussed in Chapter 4. The insights of psychology and psychotherapy should be able to help us to overcome these resistances and insecurities. For example, could the principles and techniques of transactional analysis[96] be used to encourage the replacement of the existing pattern of domination/dependence (Parent/Child) relationships in society by a new pattern of inter-dependent (Adult/Adult) relationships? Can our growing understanding of the connections between character type and work roles (for example, in business corporations where the interactions between such types as 'jungle fighters', 'company men', 'craftsmen' and 'gamesmen' have been extensively studied[97]) be applied to the interactive dynamics of a transformation process involving society as a whole? Psychologists have hardly yet begun to contribute to beneficial social change.[98]

A Multitude of Roles

The sane, humane, ecological society will be a pluralist,

polymorphous society. Its members will not aim to develop a uniform approach to life, based on a single dominant perspective or point of view — such, for example, as is implied by utilitarianism, cost/benefit analysis or attempts to improve existing methods of 'measurement of economic welfare' (MEW). It will be a society in which learning to share the perspectives of other people, other cultures, other religions, is recognised as an important aspect of personal and social growth. It will be a society which reflects the dynamic equilibrium of ecological systems in nature.

The transition to the SHE future will also be a pluralist, polymorphous process. It will reflect the processes of biological evolution, which contemporary scientists now perceive, not as an orderly progression in which one type replaces another, but as a complex flux of shifting dynamic equilibriums. Many different types of people, interacting with one another in different roles, will help to transform our existing society. Different countries will also play different parts. We need to accept the reality of this. No one's particular perspective on events or the particular field in which they are capable of making their own contribution, will be *the* one which matters. No one will be in a position to draw up a master-plan for the transition. The very idea of a master-plan for the SHE future is a contradiction in itself.

Among the people whose interactions with one another in the coming years will positively shape the process of transforming our present society into a sane, humane, ecological one, will be the following:

(1) people whose aim and skill is to speed the breakdown of the old system, by helping to make it inoperable and destroying its credibility; theirs is a *demolition* role;

(2) people who oppose proposals for change which would lead society in a hyper-expansionist or authoritarian direction; these include, for example, opponents of the spread of nuclear energy; theirs is an *opposition* role;

(3) people who are trying to improve the old system, by introducing changes which will make it better and stronger; their aim is to avert the breakdown of the old, but their actions may help to ease the transition to the new; theirs is a *reforming* role;

(4) people who are creating and developing the growth points for a new society; theirs is a *construction* role;

(5) people who aim to liberate themselves and other people from their present dependence on the existing system of society; theirs

102

is a *liberating* role;

(6)   people who are working to ensure that the old system breaks down as painlessly as possible for everyone who is dependent on it; they are managing its collapse; theirs is a *decolonising* role;

(7)   people who, as liberators or as decolonisers, are helping other people to take more control over their own lives — in health, or politics, or learning, or religion, or their economic activities, or in any other important aspect of their life; theirs is an *enabling* role;

(8)   people who are changing their personal way of life, and helping other people to change theirs, so that their lives will be more consistent with their image of a sane, humane, ecological future; theirs is a *lifestyle* role;

(9)   people who are exploring and communicating new concepts of power, wealth, work, growth, learning, healing, and so on, appropriate to a sane, humane, ecological society; they are the paradigm shifters, the ideological revolutionaries; theirs is a *metaphysical reconstruction* role;

(10)   and, finally, people who recognise that all these different sorts of people will contribute positively to the transformation of society, and who are working to make sure that the transformation, though polycentric, is a widely understood, widely shared process of conscious evolutionary change; theirs is a *strategic* role.

We should not forget other people too, whose contribution to the transformation will be negative or neutral. They include:

(11)   people who refuse to countenance the breakdown of the old system and its replacement by a new one; they will try to suppress the activities of the people listed in the previous paragraph; theirs is a *reactionary* role;

(12)   people who, having themselves failed in their own attempts to change society in one way or another are confident that no one else will succeed, and anxious that they should not; they include Nestorian wiseacres, but mainly theirs is the *pessimistic and cynical* role;

(13)   people who are humble (or superior) observers of what is happening; they enjoy talking about it, writing about it and scoring points off one another about it, but they don't want to take part; they can be helpful or unhelpful; theirs is the *academic* role;

(14)   and, finally, people who just want to get on with their own lives

in whatever circumstances happen to exist; they are not particularly concerned to encourage change or to resist it; theirs is the *routine practitioners'* role.

How will all these different sorts of people interact, as the transformation gathers pace? We cannot tell in detail in advance, but we should try to be prepared.

Different countries, as well as different individuals and groups will also have their own parts to play in the coming transformation of society.

It may have been true, as Murray Bookchin says, that every revolutionary epoch in the past has focussed upon a specific country where the social crisis was most acute — Engand in the 17th century, France in the 18th and the 19th, and Russia in the early 20th century. Moreover, there may still be an understandable tendency to think that one's own country is especially well placed to play a leading part in the impending transformation. Bookchin,[30] for example, argues that 'the center of the social crisis in the late twentieth century is the United States — an industrial colossus that produces more than half of the world's goods with little more than five percent of the world's population. Here is the Rome of world capitalism, the keystone of its imperial arch, the workshop and marketplace of its commodities, the den of its financial wizardry, the temple of its culture, and the armory of its weapons. Here, too, is the center of the world counter-revolution — and the center of the social revolution that can overthrow hierarchical society as a world-historical system. . . . America, it must be emphasised, occupies the most advanced social terrain in the world. America, more than any other country, is pregnant with the most important social crisis in history. Every issue that bears on the abolition of hierarchical society and on the construction of utopia is more apparent here than elsewhere. Here lie the resources to annul and transcend what Marx called the 'prehistory' of humanity. Here, too, are the contradictions that produce the most advanced form of revolutionary struggle.'

There are those of us, from Britain, on the other hand, who have claimed that the first industrial nation, the country of Adam Smith and Karl Marx, is now the first to reach the limits of industrialism; it is Britain, we think, that is now pioneering — reluctantly and only half-consciously perhaps — the post-industrial revolution. I sense this even more clearly now than I did five years ago. I am always struck by a paradox when I travel in the United States and in countries like Canada and Sweden. There is a greater ferment of intellectual interest there than in Britain about what the future will be like — about the possibility that modern societies may develop in radically different directions from the recent past. Reputed business thinkers at places like Stanford and Harvard have for years been teaching and writing on such topics as the changing American ideology, voluntary simplicity, and new images of man. In Ottawa, the Vanier Institute for the Family has been questioning the present view of society, and working towards an alternative perspective in which individuals, families and local communities will take pride of place. In Sweden, business thinkers and many business people are familiar with the ideas of an 'aquarian conspiracy' and a 'post-industrial' age. There is also more practical experimentation in those countries (especially, but not only, in California) with new ways of living and new forms of consciousness. The paradox is that, even if the so-called opinion formers in Britain seem much less interested, our whole society is, in fact, already struggling with the future, trying to cope in practice — if not in theory — with what happens when industrial societies come to the end of the road. In spite of all the intellectual ferment, the USA has not yet reached that stage of practical involvement; there is still much more space there — wider physical boundaries, more economic room for manoeuvre, more psychological space — if you don't like where you are in your life or your work, there is still somewhere else to go.

However, the truth is that constructive optimists in every country feel that theirs is specially well placed to take part in the evolutionary breakthrough to a new future. After all, each country, like each individual, has its own unique perspective, its very own set of problems and opportunities, hang-ups and insights. Learning to understand that other countries are likely to experience the change of direction towards the polymorphous SHE future differently from one's own, will itself be part of the change.

6
Strategy for Change

Previous chapters have discussed what the impending transformation of society might be like. This chapter is concerned with action to help to bring the transformation about.

Most of the people who actively help to bring about the transformation to the SHE future will not be doing so from a sense of duty, or because other people have told them they ought. Nor will they be obeying orders or regulations from above. They will be doing so because that is how they want to spend their lives. Learning new skills and new ways of living and working, enabling one another to become more self-reliant — these will be the kind of things they find valuable for themselves. As in the industrial revolution, or in the great surge westward across America in the 19th century, the main breakthroughs will be made by people carving out the new frontier, occupying new space for themselves, and blazing a trail for other people to follow. Some of these will be fortunate people, acting out their own choices. Others will be quite the opposite, living and working in new ways because they have no other choice. In either case, their initiatives will not come from moralisers preaching, nor from policy-makers and bureaucrats imposing a grand plan for change.[99]

There will often be room for argument whether particular activities (or people, or organisations) are part of the problem or part of the solution; do they hinder or help the transition to the SHE future? For instance, if you fly by jet-plane all over the world to tell people that they should use bicycles instead of energy-expensive transport, is your message likely to be more effective than your example, or vice versa? If you take up self-sufficient organic farming, after making a lot of money as a stockbroker, which of those two ways of life will you be an advertisement for? If you make local common ownership in industry an issue in national politics, will you be helping to decentralise economic activity or will you simply be confirming the business-as-usual processes of centralised power? Because people who are trying to create a better future have to live in the present, questions like those can be asked of almost everybody. It is probably best to ask them critically about your own activities and sympathetically about other people's, and then trust your judgement in both cases.

Egotism and cliquishness are part of the human condition. Activists for change sometimes seem especially vulnerable to them. By being too possessive about their activities, they often underestimate what other people are doing and repel their co-operation. The same thing happens on a larger scale when people identify themselves with a banner or a label or a leader. When we become members of a political party, or a professional organisation, or a trade union, or followers of Christ or Marx or some other leader or guru, we can easily become opponents to people who are marching in the same direction under another banner. Much of our energy and theirs is then siphoned off into secondary activities directed to the maintenance of our particular club or clique and to the propagation of its proprietary doctrines. Many people cannot manage without clubs and cliques and banners and labels and leaders and doctrines of this kind, but they can be very destructive. Witness the antagonisms that have so often arisen between different sections of the socialist movement.

Activists can often damage their cause by being unnecessarily threatening to other people. Alvin Toffler has made us all familiar with the concept of future shock;[13] the prospect of the future — even thinking about the future — can be frightening for many people. So if you want people to take an interest in your hopes for the future, you may have to take the trouble to calm their fears. Some sophistication is needed if, for example, vociferous opponents of nuclear power are to avoid playing into the hands of the nuclear lobby. In general, it may be tempting to try to put the fear of God into lazy, privileged, complacent, short-sighted members of the existing establishment. This can serve a useful purpose, in certain circumstances. But usually not. It should always be a matter for deliberate decision whether frightening people is likely to be helpful to what you are trying to do.

Pieces of the Action

The following suggestions are offered as a practical device for stimulating productive thought and action, and for facilitating communication. I would ask that readers experiment with them and then perhaps try to improve them, before seeking reasons to reject them out of hand. As a general rule, too much discussion about the future — especially by politicians and academics — consists of negative attempts to dispute or discredit what other people propose.

I have taken six important *transformation roles* (from among the roles enumerated in Chapter 5), and I have combined them with thirty important *activity areas*. The combination gives 180 different *transformation activities*.

The six transformation roles and thirty activity areas are listed below. An example of a transformation role is *Lifestyles;* this means changing your way of life to be more consistent with your vision of the SHE future. An example of an activity area is *Work and Employment;* this means the kind of work you do and the way you do it. Combining the Lifestyle transformation role and the Work and Employment activity area gives the following transformation activity: changing your way of life so that your work is more consistent with your vision of a desirable future.

In practice, real-life activities cannot be neatly parcelled up into 180 or any other number of different compartments. But this basic framework does — if sensibly used — provide a valuable stimulus to new thinking and action. It can also provide a context for the exchange of information about different activities on different parts of the new frontier.

The six transformation roles are as follows:

A. *Lifestyles:* changing one's personal way of life so that it is more consistent with the SHE future.

B. *Enabling (Liberation):* fostering new growth points (e.g. alternative technology, common ownership in industry, Yoga techniques) which help people to liberate themselves from dependence, to become more self-reliant, and to develop their autonomy.

C. *Enabling (Decolonisation);* managing the breakdown of existing institutions, relationships, etc., so as to help previously dependent people to become more self-reliant, and to develop their autonomy.

D. *Metaphysical Reconstruction:* creating new visions of the SHE future, developing new paradigms, and communicating them.

E. *Strategy:* mapping the transition to the SHE future; identifying pitfalls and unresolved problems; and providing opportunities for communication, information exchange, and cross-fertilisation.

F. *Opposition:* opposing and attempting to obstruct activities — such as the construction of fast-breeder nuclear reactors, or practices perpetuating racial or sex discrimination — which tend in the direction of the Business-As-Usual, Disaster, AC, or HE scenarios.

108

The thirty activity areas are as follows:
1. Families, Households and Local Communities
2. Roles of the Sexes
3. Roles of Children, Adults and the Elderly
4. Land Use and Land Tenure
5. Agriculture and Food
6. Conservation of Minerals and Materials
7. Manufacture, Repair and Maintenance of Things
8. Provision of Services and Care to People
9. Politics and Government
10. Economic Organisation
11. Management
12. Energy
13. Transport
14. Cities, Towns and Rural Resettlement
15. Housing
16. Roles of Professions
17. Science and Technology
18. Health
19. Education
20. Money and Finance
21. Work and Employment
22. Religion and Philosophy
23. Arts and Culture
24. Leisure, Entertainment and Sport
25. Information and Communications Media
26. Crime, Prisons, Police, Law, etc.
27. Animal Welfare, Wildlife, etc.
28. Third World
29. International Relations
30. Disarmament, Peace and Security.

In order to imagine the use of this conceptual framework to stimulate ideas and action, let us take some combinations at random.

A1 — Lifestyles & Families, Households and Local Communities — means changing one's way of life so as to play a more balanced part in the life of one's family, household and local community. It might, for example, include changing from a full-time to part-time job; or changing from full-time housework to a part-time local job.

F30 — Opposition & Disarmament and Peace — means acting in opposition to military expansion, weapons development, the arms

109

trade, etc, in the cause of disarmament and peace. It would apply to people in the peace movement, and to pressure group activities of an anti-military character.

B10 — Enabling (Liberation) & Economic Organisation — means acting to encourage the development (by liberation) of new forms of economic organisation which exist to serve people. It would include the activity of a group of employees who are striving to turn their enterprise into a common ownership or worker co-operative.

C10 — Enabling (Decolonisation) & Economic Organisation — means acting to encourage the development (by decolonisation) of new forms of economic organisation which exist to serve people. It would apply to the directors and managers of a large business enterprise who hived off a subsidiary part of it and enabled it to operate independently as a common ownership or worker co-operative.

D15 — Metaphysical Reconstruction & Housing — means creating and disseminating new ideas about housing, appropriate to the SHE future, as John Turner has done in his book 'Housing by People'.[87]

B26 — Enabling (Liberation) & Crime, Prisons, Police, Law, etc. — means acting to encourage decentralisation and greater personal autonomy in the field of crime, prisons, etc. Two widely different examples would be: a campaign to encourage private individuals to conveyance their own house purchases; and the activities of the Delancey Street Foundation in San Francisco, which helps criminals, drug addicts and drop-outs to rehabilitate themselves.[100]

E1 — Strategy & Families, Households and Local Communities — means helping to develop a strategy for strengthening the role in society of families, households and local communities. The work of the Vanier Institute of the Family is an example.[55]

D19 — Metaphysical Reconstruction & Education — means creating and disseminating new ideas about education, for example as Peter Abbs and Graham Carey have done in 'proposals for a New College.'[101]

D22 — Metaphysical Reconstruction & Religion and Philosophy — means creating and disseminating new ideas about religion and philosophy, as various feminist and ecological writers have done, for example.[102]

Each of the 180 transformation activities provides a useful subject for brainstorming discussion to identify as many possible ways of carrying out that activity as the participants can suggest. For instance, a discussion about energy might focus on possible examples of C12 — Enabling (Decolonisation) & Energy. Participants would be encouraged to think of all the initiatives that could be taken by governments, nationalised industries, oil companies, other businesses and industries, scientists, trade unions, etc., to enable energy users to become more self-reliant in meeting the energy needs of their households and local communities. Or in a discussion of E14 — Strategy & Cities, Towns and Rural Resettlement — people would be encouraged to think of as many ways as possible of mapping the transition from today's over-urbanised situation (with 2 per cent of working people in agriculture in a country like Britain) to a situation in 30 or 40 years' time in which 10 per cent might be working in agriculture. A game can be played in which each participant picks a transformation role out of one hat and an activity area out of an other, and brainstorms the resulting combination.

These 180 transformation activities can also be used very broadly as a basis for organising information. Through the Turning Point network and in other ways I receive information and requests for information about people and organisations who are working for the SHE future. It is not possible to organise information rigorously according to the transformation activities as described above. Most real-life activities overlap several categories. But the framework helps to suggest the shape of the new territory being opened up by a multitude of scattered pioneers and settlers — where they are in relation to one another, what they have in common, where they could go next, who is there already, and who might be able to help them on their way. It is an aid to the kind of shared strategic thinking that is needed for the transition to the SHE future.

Above all, the framework of transformation activities helps to show that the people who are actively and usefully involved in the transition to the SHE future will be doing their own thing in one or another (or several) of a multitude of different ways. It helps to convey an impression of how very wide ranging they are. It also helps to suggest an ecological model of social change. The future will be shaped by the interactions of millions of different people. Moreover, this will be a process which no-one can stand outside. Those who try to stand outside it — either to observe it, or in an effort to ignore it — will be helping (by so doing) to shape its outcome for better or for worse.[103]

Other Theories of Social Change

So the change of direction to a new, more feminine, more ecological path of development, whose main features will include decentralisation, self-reliance and mutual aid, will itself be a decentralised process, characterised by self-reliance and mutual aid, and consisting of a multiplicity of activities on the part of great numbers of different people. The means thus match the end, which is appropriate. But more than this. The polycentric, people-centred approach to creating a future society which is polycentric and people-centred is the only approach that could possibly succeed. A comparison with other theories and strategies of social change makes this quite clear.

(1) *Technological Imperative*

One school of thought believes that social change is shaped by technological change: this has been true for the past and it will stay true for the future. Whether or not he meant to give currency to this view, Marx helped to do so when he said: 'In acquiring new productive forces men change their mode of production; and in changing their mode of production, in changing the way of earning their living, they change all their social relations. The hand-mill gives you society with the feudal lord; the steam-mill, society with the industrial capitalist.'[104]

It is difficult to deny that industrial societies have been shaped by the advent of railways, electricity, automobiles, aircraft, telecommunications, computers, and so on, in ways that no one actually chose. Many people assume that this will continue into the future: new technologies will lead the way, and the question for human beings is whether or not we can adapt ourselves to the challenges that the new technologies will bring. That, for example, was the clear message of Alvin Toffler's[13] vision of a super-industrial society in 'Future Shock.' Although that vision was softened considerably in his later book 'The Third Wave,' new technology was still cast in the leading role. The same assumption has coloured most public discussion about information technology in the last few years.

It is perfectly possible that, as a matter of fact, the technological imperative will continue to call the tune — that new technologies will continue to be developed just because they can be, that people will then be persuaded to use them and adapt to them, and that they will then shape people's lives. But this domination by technology points towards disaster. And it need not happen. If it does happen, it will be by default — because we humans have failed to choose the new technologies which will give us a way of life we value.

112

So, although you may believe — as a matter of predicting what seems most probable — that technology will call the tune, this is no argument for accepting that this is how things are to be. And, although new small-scale technologies are now coming in that will encourage decentralised self-reliance and mutual aid, it would be rash to wait passively in the expectation that small-scale technology will simply waft us along the path of development we want to take.

(2) *Reformism*

If you accept that active measures are needed to shape the future of society, who is to take them? The conventional answer is: the government. In the representative democracies of the western industrialised countries, this is achieved by political lobbying and public debate, and, where larger changes are concerned, by getting a new government elected with a commitment to put the desired measures through.

This reformist approach, so the conventional view maintains, has stood the test of time in those countries which have progressed successfully over the years without violent revolution. The development of 19th and 20th century Britain, from the great Reform Bill of 1832 to the post-war Welfare State of 1945, is often quoted as an example. Many people's automatic thought about developments they would like to see (and their response to events they do not like) is that 'the government should do something about it.' Many people take it for granted that government provides a society with its mechanism of social change.

I used to take that view. But my experience of working in and with government for twenty years led me to change my mind, and subsequent reflection helped me to understand why the situation today is different from what it may have been in the 19th and early 20th centuries.

I learned that government organisations, like other organisations, are more interested in themselves than in the people they exist to serve. I became familiar with the short-sightedness which dominates them and the inertia in which they are interlocked. I became aware that, although their first purpose is to preserve themselves and the interests of the people who work in them, their ways of working make them so resistant to change that they are scarcely capable of reform even in their own self-interest. They will only accept change, and then as little and as slowly as possible, when it has become inescapably obvious to everybody that change is unavoidable and indeed overdue. This means

113

that reforms introduced through government are bound to be too little and too late, never properly planned, always contested and muddled. This is doubly true of progressive change, since political parties, government departments and the powerful commercial, professional and trade union lobbies that bring pressure to bear on the processes of government, reflect the status quo. Within the status quo they may compete with one another, but they all want to maintain the existing power structure broadly as it is, since their own power and position derive from it.

Why, then, is the present situation different from that which existed in the 19th and early 20th centuries? The answer is that at that time progress coincided with organisational growth. Up to the middle of the 20th century the generic interest of political parties, government agencies, business corporations, trade unions and professions such as medicine and teaching — that is to say the interest which they all shared as organisations seeking growth for themselves and expanded opportunities for the people who worked in them — coincided with the general direction of social progress, including parliamentary reform, the growth of mass political parties, the expansion first of government regulation and then of the welfare state, the growth of big business organisations and the rise of trade union power. So long as that coincidence continued, the processes of evolutionary reform were carried forward by a powerful underlying momentum, with long-term results that now tend to obscure how muddled were the actual changes made on each particular occasion, e.g. in respect of the Corn Laws or the Poor Law. Today, however, that direction of social and economic progress has reached its limit. A complete change of direction is needed now, leading to a decline in the role of mass political parties, government agencies, business corporations and so on. It is quite unrealistic to expect a process of evolutionary reform, arising mainly from the interplay of political forces corresponding to the existing power structure, to bring about such a change of direction. Such a change will have to be initiated primarily by people outside the existing power structure, who identify with the new direction of change.[105]

(3) Political Revolution

Justifiable impatience with the reformist approach pushes many people towards a more aggressive strategy of social change.

Some opt for political revolution. They agree with the reformers about the central importance of the state as the main instrument of

114

social change, but they disagree with the reformers about how to get the state to carry out the policies they want. Instead of operating through the processes of electioneering, lobbying and parliamentary debate, they aim to take over the state by force.

Revolutions of this kind have included the French Revolution and the Russian Revolution. But such a revolution could not be successfully carried out by progressive forces in a major industrialised country today. (The possibility of a right wing coup to secure the status quo — as has happened in Hungary, Czechoslovakia, and Poland in recent decades — is another matter altogether. So is the possibility of a progressive revolution in a third world country such, for example, as Castro's Cuba.) Moreover, as the outcome of the Russian Revolution suggests, even if any such revolution were carried out, its consequences are unlikely to be progressive. We will return to these points in the context of the Marxist approach.

(4) *Confrontation and Direct Political Action*

Other people opt for direct, or extra-parliamentary, political action. Some undertake this in order to undermine the normal processes of government, as part of a strategy for political revolution. Others undertake it to reinforce the more constitutional activities of electioneering, lobbying and parliamentary debate, with the aim of electing a new government or of persuading the existing one to carry out new policies. Direct political action normally takes the form of opposition, protest, obstruction — including strikes, picketing and other varieties of industrial action. It can also take a violent form, the most obvious of these being political terrorism.

Direct political action may have a valuable part to play in the transition to a SHE future, for example by opposing nuclear power, nuclear weapons and cruel treatment of animals, and by trying to prevent damage to local communities by juggernaut lorries, and the destruction and pollution caused by new roads, factories or airports. But two reservations must be made.

First, direct activists can often play into the hands of their opponents. They often present themselves or are shown by the media as negative and irresponsible, as congenital trouble-makers or naive do-gooders — impractical, unconstructive, self-indulgent, if not deliberately destructive.

The second reservation is more fundamental. The prevailing perception of politics as a sphere of adversarial activity connected with the functions of the state and quite separate from the ways in which most of us actually live and work in our normal daily life, can give this kind of confrontational, direct action — for example, a 'march for jobs' — a deceptive aura of significance and glamour. The mass media, deeply rooted as they are in the status quo, cultivate this deception and thereby help to distract our attention from the more effective kinds of direct action that each of us could take. I refer to positive, constructive — but often not superficially glamorous — steps to change the way we ourselves live and work and relate to other people and the world around us. By that kind of direct action we actually can change and improve the part of society which, by our behaviour and way of life, we ourselves help to create.

Objections to a Pluralist Strategy

Two main objections have been made to the pluralist strategy for social transformation put forward in this book. Both are about power. One is concerned with the feasibility of liberation, the other with the feasibility of decolonisation. They are, in other words, opposite sides of the same coin.

The idea that people will be able to liberate themselves from dependence on the big system and organisations and professions of late industrial society has been said to imply a liberal conception of the human being and social relations: the individual is a fairly powerful entity, possessing a fair amount of freedom, who can exert influence in the realm of ideas. This is quite plausible from a middle-class vantage-point, but it makes very little sense from that of about 50 per cent of the population of a nation such as Britain. The Left, therefore, has generally dubbed such conceptions 'bourgeois idealism' — meaning, in effect, a projection from the bourgeois' own place in society. Instead, it has advised us to take very seriously the huge differences in power and in material interests between the classes in society; and it looks for radical social change, not through the work of individuals in 'transformation roles,' but through the concerted action of a whole class. Even though such action may bring about some hurt, the argument is that it is the only way that the 'class conflict' can be won.[106]

Similarly, the idea that people enjoying positions of power and status will be prepared to decolonise the systems which give them those positions, and give their power away, is also said to be naive and utopian. No one ever willingly gives power away, according to this view; if politicians, trade union leaders, professional people and managers of multinational companies are to lose their power, it will

116

have to be taken from them.

These are weighty objections. But, as I shall suggest, they are not as conclusive as they may seem.

However, it is almost certainly correct that so-called middle-class people will play a big part in the post-industrial revolution. They have been prominent in every important revolution in the past, including the American, French, and Russian revolutions and, of course, the industrial revolution. Non-conforming people in the middle ranges of society are less deeply committed to the status quo than more privileged members of the establishment. At the same time, circumstances often give more freedom to them than to so-called working-class people to take up new initiatives and socially transformative roles. So, if the distinction between middle-class and working-class could still be insisted upon, it probably would make sense to argue — callously, I agree — that the post-industrial revolution is likely to be pioneered by middle-class people; the representatives of working-class interests probably will stay bogged in the arguments and controversies, hopes and fears, of the industrial age which is passing away; and, in due course, working class people probably will find themselves with no alternative to adapting to the new conditions which they have had little part in shaping — just as happened at the beginning of the industrial age.

But, in fact, the 19th century distinction between bourgeoisie and proletariat no longer applies. Many so-called working-class people today are more practical, more resourceful and readier to branch out than people who only have obsolescent white-collar skills and are inhibited by middle-class values of security and status. Objectively the gap between the way of life and standard of living of middle-class and working-class people is nothing like as wide as it was. More importantly, we almost all now share the same subjective sense of personal smallness and powerlessness in an institutionalised world. This is the prime cause of most people's helplessness, inertia and inability to act today. The concept of person power, combining self-reliance with mutual aid, is relevant for almost everyone in the kind of society we have today, whether they think of themselves as middle- or working-class.

So let us turn to the second objection. Why should people who now have power become willing to give it away? The answer is simple. They may be willing to give it away, as parents do to their children. Otherwise, they will only give it away when they recognise they have to. And when will this be? There are only two possibilities. It will

117

either be when someone else becomes strong enough to take power away from them from above. Or it will be when those upon whom their power rests — their dependents, customers, employees, clients — withdraw support from below. The first possibility is the one on which the Marxists focus their strategy for revolution and social transformation. The second is more likely to be effective.

Comparison with Marxism[107]

There are important parallels between Marx's vision of the transformation of 19th century bourgeois capitalism into a communist society and the prospect — put forward in this book — of a transformation of late 20th century industrialism into a sane, humane, ecological (SHE) society. There are crucial differences too.

As Marx pointed out, the prevailing economic and social relations between people in a society correspond to the stage of development which that society has reached. As he put it, "The sum total of these relations of production constitutes the economic structure of society, on which rises a legal and political superstructure, and to which correspond definite forms of social consciousness."[108] He saw that every society contained inherent — and, as we might now say, escalating — contradictions in its existing structure of relations, which would eventually lead to its collapse. The future would thus contain a qualitative break. A new kind of society would come into existence. A new epoch would be born. This applied to ancient society and to feudal society and it would apply, so Marx said, to the capitalist or bourgeois society of the 19th century. Today it applies to late industrial society in which the escalating contradictions of the formal economy herald its collapse and the advent of the post-industrial revolution.

For a transformation (or revolution) of this kind to occur, Marx recognised that not only must the objective circumstances have developed to the right point, but the subjective condition must also have arisen. In other words there must be widespread consciousness of the nature of the situation and of the action needed to transform it. He identified alienation as an important ingredient in this widespread growth of consciousness — alienation meaning that people realise they are used as mere commodities in the kind of society that currently exists. He saw that those who are thus alienated from the dominant values of their society will eventually form a large section of it, and that they will be drawn together by consciousness that they share a common condition.

118

As the contradictions in the existing structure of economic and social relations become more acute, Marx argued, powerful social forces will polarise around two conflicting sets of interests and two contrasting visions of the future. The dominant set of interests will be enforced by the dominant section of society. The opposing set of interests and a new vision of the future will be developed by the alienated section of society, which the dominant section has brought into existence in opposition to itself. The sharpening conflict between these two sets of interests will provide the motor force for the revolution that is to come.

Up to this point the Marxist analysis is helpful. It helps to illuminate what the post-industrial revolution will involve and what will help to bring it about. The dominant thrust of industrial society has created a hyperexpansionist (HE) vision of the future. The proponents of this vision have now brought into existence against themselves a growing movement in support of a saner, more humane, more ecological (SHE) society. The conflict between these two interests will provide the motor force for the post-industrial revolution.

It is here that we run into the first crucial difference between the 19th century situation which Marx knew and the situation which exists today. The basic conflict in late industrial society is no longer between the bourgeoisie and the proletariat. The structure of relations between people who own the means of production and people who sell their labour has changed fundamentally in the past hundred years. Almost every inhabitant today of a country like Britain, for example, is an owner of the means of production, through insurance companies, pension funds and the nationalised industries; and at the same time the majority of active people, including many of the most powerful in the land, are now paid employees. There is still a struggle, and a vital one, but it is no longer between one class of capitalist owners and another class of propertyless employees. The successors today of those two 19th century classes are the elements of society which identify with the dominant, masculine, technocratic, institutional, (HE) vision of the future and those which, having emerged in opposition to them, want to create the SHE society. It is these new opponents whose conflict is, as I say, beginning to provide the motor force for the post-industrial revolution. The practical questions today are about conflict between SHE and HE, not about conflict between the proletariat and the bourgeoisie.

The second crucial difference between the Marxist analysis and that put forward here concerns the role of the state.

According to Marx the state's main function was to provide the ruling class with an instrument of control and, in the last resort, of violence with which to dominate the rest of society. From this, Marx argued, it followed that the revolutionary class must first take over the state. Then they must turn it into their own instrument for dominance and control, and use it to effect the revolutionary transformation of the old form of society into the new. That transformation would consist of rooting out the remains of the previous ruling class, eliminating the class antagonisms surviving from their period of dominance, and enabling a new society — a new set of social and economic relationships — to emerge 'in which the free development of each is the condition for the free development of all.' The emergence of that new society would permit, and at the same time require, the state to wither away. In my terminology the state would be expected to decolonise itself. It would give away its powers over people, and enable people to exercise power for themselves.

The key point to note is that the Marxist transformation of society is to be a two-stage process, with the state playing a centrally important role in each stage. (In practice, Marxists have been mainly concerned with the first stage: how is the revolutionary class to take over the state and establish its own rule?)

We can agree on two points with Marxist thinking about the state. First, the state does indeed reflect, and aim to perpetuate, the prevailing structure of economic and social relations. Like all institutions the state is, in cybernetic terms, 'programmed to produce itself.'[109] It is 'dynamically conservative.'[110] Second, the transformation of the state, so that much of it withers away and dissolves in a form of society in which the freer development of each person will create conditions for the freer development of all, will indeed be a feature of the post-industrial revolution. But there are also two vital points of difference. First, what is the state today, and can it be taken over? Second, what is the most realistic approach to withering it away?

The state in late industrial society is very different from the 19th century state of Marx's time. The state must now be understood as a very wide-ranging system of interlocking institutions. Parliament, judiciary, central government, local government, public corporations and nationalised industries, business corporations, financial institutions, trade unions, health services, education services, welfare services, the media and the professions — this whole institutional structure has to be included in the concept of the state today.

Moreover, in our various roles as workers, customers, students, taxpayers, patients, pensioners and so on, almost everyone has now become part of this expanded state. Are we now to take over ourselves? What would such a takeover involve, and how could it be carried out? Could those who now run these institutions all be replaced? Could their replacements all be centrally controlled? Even if they could, what would this be expected to achieve?

It is very difficult to see how a revolutionary takeover of the state as the first stage in a progressive transformation of late industrial society could possibly be carried out. So what about the second stage? Assuming, hypothetically, that a revolutionary takeover had been accomplished, what prospect would there be of the state withering away?

As I said, Marxists have not given much attention to the practicalities of this. And, in fact, it is here that a damaging contradiction in the Marxist theory of social transformation raises its head. Marxists argue that the people who have power at present will not give their power away unless it is taken from them by force. But they offer no evidence to suggest that people who had succeeded in a revolutionary takeover of the state would behave any differently. Why should we suppose that those people would be any more able and willing to give up power than the people they had replaced? Such evidence as there is, for example in Soviet Russia, suggests that they would not. A strategy for social transformation which relies on the hope that they would is little more than utopian wishful thinking.

In fact, this central weakness of the Marxist strategy for social transformation is the central weakness of late industrial society in every sphere — its instrumentalism. The assumption is made that, in order to create a better society, something quite different — the takeover of the state — must be accomplished first. Like those who want to postpone the creation of social wellbeing until economic growth has been achieved, the Marxists want to postpone creating a better society until they have achieved the intermediate, instrumental goal of taking over the state. Means are given priority over the end. In due course, means replace the end. Eventually, achievement of the means is sought in ways that positively damage the prospect of achieving the end.

A more realistic approach, a more realistic model for social transformation, must be based on a one-stage, as opposed to a two-stage, strategy for withering away — or at least cutting down to size — the complex of institutions which comprise the extended state in late industrial societies. It must aim directly for the real goal (i.e. the withering away), and cut out the distracting, intermediate, instrumental goal (i.e. the taking over). It must offer the prospect of constructive action of many different kinds to many different kinds of people, which will reduce their dependence on the extended state and thus contribute directly to transforming society. As I have said, this kind of direct action will not be primarily of an oppositional, confrontational kind. That will often be needed. But the primary need will be for positive action by people directly to change their own way of living for the better and by so doing to create a better society around them.

Non-Violent Transformation[111]

To conclude, then, I do not suggest that the technological imperative will cease to operate altogether; there will still be technological changes to which we shall have to adapt. Nor do I suppose that government can be ignored; there will be changes of policy and regulation to be made in many fields. Nor, again, do I say that direct political action of an oppositional kind will be unnecessary; there are likely to be many occasions for it. What I do believe is that the post-industrial revolution will be brought about primarily as a non-violent transformation of society in which there will be a constructive role for almost everyone to play.

The post-industrial revolution can happen this way because industrialised society is breaking down and because people are beginning to see a better alternative to it. It can happen this way as more and more people begin to understand that, by liberating themselves from excessive dependence on the system of institutions which industrialised society has created, they can enjoy better lives themselves and help other people to do the same.

In every department of our lives there is a multitude of ways we can begin — many have already begun — to liberate ourselves and one another. There is no need to try to destroy the present system or take it over. It will be enough to withdraw support from it: to work rather less in the paid job, and rather more at unpaid work at home and in the local neighbourhood; to spend rather less money on food, or repairs, or entertainment, and to give rather more time to growing food, doing repairs, and creating entertainment for yourself, your family and your neighbours; to give rather less time and attention to remote forms of politics, and rather more time and energy to local issues that affect the life of yourself and your friends and your neighbours more closely; and so on.

Only the naive would suppose that everyone in dominant positions will be eager to give their power away, or that everyone in dependent positions will be eager to liberate themselves. Domination is what provides a sense of security and self-worth for some people; dependence is what provides it for others. The SHE vision of the post-industrial future will be rejected by both these types. As its prospect becomes more likely, the possibility of mass psychosis among them, leading to new forms of fascism, is not be be ignored. Some will do all they can to create the HE future, with its dominant technocratic elite and its dependent, irresponsible masses. Others will try to impose something like a police state.

But there is reason for hope. As industrialised society reaches its limits and begins to break down, more and more people in managerial and professional positions are beginning to feel imprisoned in worthless roles. They find it less easy to help, or to dominate, those who are supposed to be dependent on them. They begin to yearn for a more convivial, more familial, more neighbourly life for themselves. They begin to see that their own liberation depends on giving their positional power away. They begin to want to help their customers or their clients to be less dependent on them. They begin to think about the changes and reforms that will be necessary in order to decolonise their part of the power structure. As these people decide to change the direction of their own lives, they will be deciding to change the structure of relations in society. It is of such changes in self and society that the post-industrial revolution will be made.

In spite of its parallels with the Marxist approach, this will seem an unglamorous prospect for many people, especially men, who have acquired a taste for the ways of life that go with working for the conventional kind of political revolution or social reform. Conditioned to suppose, as I once was, that the power to initiate social change lies in the so-called corridors of power, they will see the direct action of transformation activities as 'dropping out'. It all depends on your perception of reality, of course. The real drop-outs, it now seems to me, are the people who devote their lives to the institutional superstructures of a form of society that is passing away.

As the traditional revolutionary and reformist approaches continue to lose credibility as strategies for transforming society, so a new consciousness is emerging in opposition to the dominant values and assumptions of the late industrial age, on which those revolutionary and reformist approaches have been based. It is a consciousness of being deprived and dehumanised, just as Marx described. But it is also a consciousness of how much we impose this deprivation and dehumanisation on ourselves. It is a consciousness that we can act to liberate ourselves and one another. It is a consciousness that more and more of us can move in this same direction without someone else having to organise us; and that political parties and manifestos, as instruments for organising collective action, belong to the factory mentality of the industrial age. It is a consciousness that we are part of a growing movement to create a saner, more humane, more ecological future. It is this consciousness that defines what Marx, if he were alive today, would call the new revolutionary class.

POSTSCRIPT TO CHAPTER SIX

In order to keep this revised edition reasonably short, I have not attempted to deal in any depth with issues that were not covered in the original text. But I do want to touch briefly on two issues that have come up often in discussion and correspondence. They raise important questions about an effective strategy for change. One concerns the best way of working for international security, peace and disarmament. The other is feminism.

Peace

A securely peaceful world society will only be created if we change the present direction of development and the present system of dominant values. Only when our patterns of living become more decentralised, more self-reliant, more ecological, shall we become less threatening to, and less threatened by, people in other parts of the world. Institutional values will have to give way to personal values, masculine values to feminine values, exploitative values to ecological values. In the long run, helping to bring about these changes directly within our own personal spheres of influence will be the most effective way for most of us to help improve the prospects for a positively peaceful world.

So far as more immediate action to reduce the risk of catastrophic war is concerned, there is no simple answer. The governmental, industrial, scientific and military establishments of the world are unlikely to halt the arms race and create positive peace, if they are simply allowed to proceed with multilateral international negotiations at their own pace. On the other hand, a premature collapse of existing arrangements for international security, such as might be precipitated by immediate unilateral disarmament, would be very dangerous too.

What is needed is for people, acting as international peace people, to begin to withdraw the power and resources we now give to the military-industrial complex in every country of the world, and to bring pressure on all governments to move in a peaceful direction.

The practicalities of this will be very difficult. But it is the only realistic way to proceed. Steps of this kind are being taken already by sections of the peace movement[112]. In this sphere, as in others, the aim must be to liberate ourselves from institutional domination. By thus withdrawing the power we now give to governments, the military, the arms industry and the scientific establishment we should seek to compel them, not to collapse in chaos, but to decolonise themselves in reasonably good order, as is discussed in Chapter 5. How can we get enough people world-wide to join together in this endeavour? This is not a rhetorical question implying that we should forget the whole idea. It is a practical question. It urges people of goodwill to find practical answers to it.

Feminism

The idea that the future will be shaped by a shift from masculine to feminine values, and from institutional to personal ways of doing and being, is threatening to many men. We have been conditioned to commit ourselves to the formal structures of society out there. To be told that these are becoming less important than the more personal side of life, in which we feel less at home, is damaging to our ego. The redundant executive symbolises our vulnerability.

But the same idea is also threatening to many feminist women. Their goal is to get on equal terms with men in the world as it is today. They distrust anyone — especially a man — who says that higher priority should be given to feminising the world than to achieving equality between men and women in the masculine world that actually exists. They suspect him of trying to defuse their militancy. This is understandable.

In fact, it is probably not very helpful for men to suggest what particular roles women should aim to play in the transition to a SHE future.[113] More to the point is for men to learn to liberate ourselves, as women have been doing, from the particular kinds of dependency to which we have been reduced in late industrial societies. We need to free ourselves from the insecurities and practical helplessness which habitually lead us to seek continuing achievement of a formal kind — earnings, status, promotion and all the other varieties of institutionalised good marks for grown-up boys — and to need the reassurance of patriarchal relationships with women. Liberating ourselves and thereby helping to create a society in which women and men share much more equally than today the rewards and the responsibilities of both the formal and the informal side of life, is our proper role in the ecology of social change.

7
Tea-Time at Marshbeck: Looking Back from 2050

It is the afternoon of 5th January, 2050. A few days ago the 21st century reached the half-way mark. The occasion has made people think. They are still talking about the New Year celebrations, and the various ideas about the past and the future that came up.

Emily Malik, Eskimo Johnson, and their two children, Bruno (aged eight) and Shantih (aged six), are a typical English family group. Their way of life is typical too. They live in a village (called Marshbeck) a few miles from a town centre (called Trentside) about a hundred and fifty miles from London.

Emily and Eskimo originally came to Marshbeck as a result of a contact made through the LHP. A house and work-role had become vacant and the members of the cluster concerned were seeking a new family group to take the place of the people who had left. (As they were reminded during the New Year celebrations, their grandparents and great grandparents seventy years ago did not have LHPs — 'leisure, home and personal' informatic sets linked to the worldwide networks. The possibility of combining telephones, television sets and computer terminals had long been foreseen, but it was not until after 1990 that LHPs began to come in as standard domestic equipment. Similarly, it was not until the '90s that clusters of houses owned in common by the residents came in as a regular form of home occupation and neighbourhood living, after the final breakdown of the old money system had brought publicly provided housing virtually to an end and put personal house purchase out of most people's reach.

Emily's and Eskimo's predecessors at Marshbeck has been invited to move to PISCES (the Pacific Inter-Species Communication and Empathy School) in Tahiti to work out their growing commitment to the marine consciousness movement. The cluster needed someone to take their house who would also take responsibility for managing the minifarm. This suited Emily well, and Eskimo discovered that the biodegradable plastics and recycling unit in Trentside would give him three days work a week, monitoring their automated quality control. He also found that the Marshbeck community health centre would be an ideal place to develop his capacities as a healer. So Emily and Eskimo visited Marshbeck and met the residents of the cluster. Then both sides made a few enquiries, agreement was quickly reached, and the newcomers moved in and took up their share in the common ownership. That was about five years ago.

Their cluster is a little smaller than the average. It covers about six acres. The minifarm occupies three. Buildings and private houses occupy the rest. There are three other family houses, two four-room bungalows for elderly people, one of which is shared by three people and the other by two, and a teenagers' mess (containing six bedsitters, a common room, kitchen and shower room). In addition to the teenagers' mess and the sheds for the minifarm, other shared buildings contain: the deep-freeze units; food-processing equipment (for making breads, meats, jams, chutneys, cheeses, wines, beers, and so on); the laundry; and a repair and maintenance workshop with tools for repairing clothes, household furniture and equipment, minifarm equipment, electronic and electrical equipment, bicycles and other vehicles, and buildings. There is also a copice, a small communications and operations office with informatic facilities more sophisticated than the ordinary living room LHPs. Several of the cluster's residents use the copice for their work: for example, Harley Jones does environmental and architectural consultancy; Sheelah Mackenzie calculates personalised diet and exercise optimisations; and Pik Musgrove puts together multi-media skill-tranfer packs.

It is Pik, in fact, who — with his nineteen-year-old daughter Indira and her friend Herbert from Lagos — has dropped in on Emily and Eskimo this afternoon. Harley Jones' mother, Meg, an elderly widowed lady who shares one of the bungalows, is also there. Pik is a recent widow; Marika, his partner, died last summer after an accident at a solar-powered bike-plane show in Arizona. Indira met Herbert during her community service last year at a biotechnics centre in China, where they learned to use bacteriological techniques in urban horticulture. They came back together by round-the-world windship just before Christmas.

Herbert remarks how strange it is that in England mid-afternoon is still called 'tea-time' and mid-morning is still called 'coffee-time,' although it must be thirty or forty years since people living outside the tea- and coffee-growing areas of the world have drunk tea and coffee regularly. Emily doesn't find this surprising; surely, she says, one of the functions of language is to reassure us that things haven't changed all that much; later generations use the same words as earlier ones,

128

and don't recognise that what the words refer to is something quite new.

Pik has recently been doing historical research with the Trentside Community Communications Society for their contribution to New Year's Eve Worldwide. 'Yes,' he says, 'and I think this is especially true of the last sixty or seventy years. The biggest changes that have taken place since the 1980s, when the great transformation gathered speed, have been intangible changes — changes in what some of our grandparents used to call "software," meaning people's ways of thinking, communicating and organising. The deep, unspoken priorities have changed. It's difficult now to imagine how things must have been when life for most people was empty of meaning — before they were seized, as we are, by the commitment to develop our potential as persons, in society, as part of planet Earth. Everything must have seemed quite different for them — much emptier, you would think — and yet they used the same words — like sane, humane and ecological — as we do to refer to those aspects of life.'

Emily interrupts, 'Yes, and human potential is another good example. A lot of people used to think that developing human potential meant escaping to places like ashrams in India or beaches in California. There was even a "human potential movement." Whereas we now take it for granted that developing our potential as humans means living our ordinary daily lives in creative, productive, enriching ways, including our relationships with other people and the natural world around us.'

Indira chips in, 'Those old people must have seen what was coming, don't you think? After all, history makes it pretty obvious that by the early '80s a change of direction was taking place. Here in England they had celebrated the bicentenary of the Industrial Revolution — two hundred years of fantastic progress on the material side of life — and all their good writers and thinkers had begun to discuss what post-industrial society was going to be like — the "coming age of human growth," "psycho-social invention and innovation," "personal self-development in an eco-planetary culture," and so on — maybe they still felt a bit awkward with these concepts and phrases, but their vision corresponded more or less to what actually happened.'

'That's not correct historically, you know,' says Eskimo. 'We tend to remember now only the people who got it more or less right, and whose books and recordings still have something interesting to say to us. But most of the experts and spokespeople seventy years ago were firmly imprisoned in an altogether different set of assumptions. Take

129

a simple example, which I happen to know about. Many people, like me, have a natural capacity for healing, in the same way as many people have aptitudes for swimming, or music, or whatever. No-one today doubts that most people have some capacity for healing which can be trained and developed with practice. But in the early '80s almost all the accepted people in medicine and science, including medical and scientific writers, ignored or rejected it. It wasn't until about 1990 that they really began to take it seriously and to train healers in a big way. It was then, of course, that they began to conquer the killer diseases of industrial society like cancer.'

'Exactly the same was true of economics,' Pik says. 'You have to put on a different mindset to understand what people then thought economics was about. It's fascinating to hear and watch the speeches and discussions on the old tapes and videos. Even in the late '70s and early '80s one of the main aims — this is what "full employment" meant — was that as many people as possible should work away from their homes, and should do their work for people and organisations, and on tasks, unconnected with their own lives. That seems crazy to us, I know. But for people then "employment," "unemployment," "jobs" and so on, were passionately important. Some historians of the transformation argue that all the debate and discussion about that kind of economics was just a complex tangle of empty quibbles and sophistries, with which the ambitious and clever people blinded the rest and achieved power and privilege for themselves. But the riots of the 1980s showed that these questions were real and relevant to people's lives. It must have been a bit like the theological debates (how many angels can stand on the point of a pin? and all that) which mattered so much to people six or seven hundred years ago and then seemed such nonsense as soon as the Middle Ages were over.'

'I suppose all this was connected,' says Herbert, 'with what we see as the over-masculine psyche of people at that time. I mean, they always wanted to push outwards and spend their energies on someone else's patch, not on their own — working in jobs outside their home, sending their children out to school, trading with people in other countries, converting people with different beliefs, sorting out other people's problems instead of their own. It was only about sixty years ago, you know, that people in the so-called "developed" countries realised that putting their own way of living on a permanently sustainable footing was the most effective way of helping people in the "less developed" countries to do the same. When my grandfather joined the Nigerian representatives at the U.N. just over fifty years ago, the old hands were still recalling the panic which had hit the place in the late 1980s when that simple fact began to sink in.'

'Let's be fair to them, though', Emily says. 'The great transformation didn't take place suddenly, out of the blue. Indira's right. People had been discussing alternative futures for some time. Would it be Business As Usual? Disaster? Police State? We once retrieved some of the debates from the archive data bank through the LHP. And surely, Herbert, there was the big controversy in the '80s about masculine and feminine values, and whether the post-industrial future was going to be HE or SHE.'

Old Meg Jones can keep silent no longer. 'This is all very interesting, Emily', she says, 'but the biggest thing that changed was politics. It's only about fifty years since most people realised that politics was about how you lived your own life. Then they began to do politics for themselves. When I was young in the '80s and '90s, a few thousand full-time politicians did politics for everyone else, mainly in places like Washington and Moscow, London and Brussels. They made a profession of it, a career. My mother was in the game herself for a while. She was an MP. And Herbert's quite right; I remember her saying it was a very masculine game, even for women. For most people politics meant casting a vote from time to time. That was it. The politicians liked it, of course. It gave them a lot of attention, and made them feel really important. No-one would want to go back to that now. But imagine how exciting it was at election time. Everyone stayed at home to watch the results on television. In fact, as that way of doing politics began to break down, it turned into an entertainment like horse-jumping and all the other spectator sports of those days. It must be difficult for you young people to realise what it was like, with everyone sitting passively in front of the television all the time, watching and listening to the performers. Ordinary people couldn't communicate directly with each other all over the world as you do today through the LHP'.

'Talking of politics,' says Emily, 'it's nearly six o'clock, and time we all went to the monthly cluster meeting. There won't be many domestic matters on the agenda this time, though I want to get the minifarm roster settled for the year and I think your Harley wants to propose up-grading the copice, doesn't he, Meg? But there are some external questions to discuss: what should be done about the dispute over the Marshbeck water supply? what do we think of the proposal that Trentside District should stop trying to be self-sufficient in energy? do we have any ideas for this year's inter-continental exchange programme? and shall we take up the idea of a special link with the dolphin group at PISCES? Come on Bruno and Shantih. We want a full quorum of under-tens at the cluster meeting; the voice of the future must be heard. Anyhow, we don't want people saying you're missing your education. They might suggest we send you out to school!'

Appendix

Some Questions for Discussion

Chapter 1
Which of the five scenarios — Business As Usual, Disaster, Authoritarian Control, HE and SHE — do you think is: the most probable; the most desirable? Do you think there are any other scenarios or possibilities for the future that are more probable or desirable than these five?

Chapter 2
(1) Which of the five kinds of limits to conventional economic growth do you think are most important — physical, social, institutional, psychological, conceptual? Do you think there are any other important limits?

(2) Which of the ten features of the SHE economic path do you think is most important? Do you think there are any other important features?

Chapter 3
(1) In which half of the dual economy, formal or informal, do you personally spend too much (or too little) time and energy?

(2) Why do you dislike (or like) the traditional assumption that men's work is in the formal economy and women's work in the informal economy?

(3) If we are to aim for a better balance between formal and informal activities, and a fairer distribution of both kinds of activity among people, at what level do you think changes are most needed: household, neighbourhood, district, region, nation, world?

Chapter 4
What changes in other important concepts — e.g. health, education, welfare, politics, peace — would correspond to the changes in wealth, power, growth and work discussed in this chapter?

Chapter 5
Are you personally more concerned with changes in society, or with changes in yourself and other people close to you? Do you think the links between the two kinds of change are important, or not?

Chapter 6
(1) Which of the six transformation roles most appeal to you? And in which of the thirty activity areas are you working, or would you like to work, for change?

133

(2) Objections can be made to every strategy or theory of social change — technological imperative; reformism; political revolution; confrontation and direct political action; Marxism; and the pluralist, non-violent transformation proposed in this book. Which objections seem to you to be most compelling? Do you have answers to any of them?

Chapter 7
This chapter gives only a tiny glimpse into a possible future. What important aspects of life in AD 2050 — e.g. joys, sorrows, anxieties, conflicts, failures, hopes, successes — do you think it ignores?

References and Bibliography

Note: Space precludes listing the multitude of regular publications and journals relevant to a sane, humane, ecological future. Some are mentioned below. Others include the following: Association of Humanistic Psychology newsletters (U.S.A.), Ecologist (Britain), Gandhi Marg (India), Manas (U.S.A.), Rain (U.S.A.), Resurgence (Britain). In the national press Harford Thomas' weekly column in The Guardian (Britain) stands out.

1. The first edition was written in 1977 during a part-time attachment at Loughborough University of Technology. This was organised by Gurth Higgin, Professor of Continuing Management Education there, from whose own work I learned much. See 32, 95.

2. Turning Point is an international network of people whose individual concerns range widely — environment, sex equality, third world, peace and disarmament, community politics, appropriate technology and alternatives in economics, health, education, agriculture, religion, etc. — but who share a common feeling that humankind is at a turning point. For information write to Turning Point, Spring Cottage, 9 New Road, Ironbridge, Shropshire TF8 7AU.

3. For details, see p.ii. Robert Buntz, of River Basin, organised a seven-week speaking tour of the United States for me in 1980, following publication of the American edition. (My contact with Rob Buntz was due to Bill and Margaret Ellis and their invaluable TRANET newsletter — see 52.)

4. Dr. F. H. Tyler, then Dean of the Faculty of Social Welfare, University of Calgary, Alberta, Canada, arranged my attachment there in March 1979. This stimulated my paper 'What Comes After The Welfare State? A Post-Welfare Development Path For The U.K.', given at a conference on 'Welfarism — What Now?' in Stockholm in August 1980, later published in *Futures,* February 1982.

5. This project, jointly organised by the Intermediate Technology Development Group, 9 King Street, London WC2E 8HN and the British Association for the Advancement of Science, led to a symposium on 'Technology Choice And The Future Of Work'. Full proceedings were published by BAAS, Fortress House, 23 Savile Row, London W1X 1AB. For summaries see *New Scientist,* 23rd November 1978.

6. This project, jointly organised by the American Assembly of Collegiate Schools of Business and the European Foundation for Management

Development, is reported in 'Management For The 21st Century', Kluwer-Nijhoff, 1982.

As the industrial age comes towards an end and business civilisation declines, the resulting challenges to management and industry are beginning to be faced in many countries. Among the people whose work has helped my thinking on these topics are: Peter Challen of the South London Industrial Mission; Gustav Delin, Sven Atterhed and Lennart Boksjo of the Foresight Group, Sweden; Georges Gueron and his fellow Conseillers de Synthese, Paris; Francis Kinsman of the Business Network, London; Prof. James E. Moore, then of the University of Texas, Dallas; Prof. John Morris and Hugh Gunz, Manchester Business School; Philip Sadler, Ashridge Management Centre; Goran Wiklund and his colleagues at Pedagogik and Produktion, Sweden.

Apart from many seminars and discussions with particular companies and organisations, I have been glad of opportunities to discuss the future with national and international management conferences in Denmark, Norway, Sweden and Switzerland, and with the Australian Management Association in Brisbane — this last in the course of a rewarding two-week speaking tour of Australia in 1980, arranged by Don Benjamin and his fellow New South Wales humanists.

7. My report on 'Another Britain' was circulated with IFDA Dossier 6, April 1979, by the International Foundation for Development Alternatives, 2 Place du Marche, 1260 Nyon, Switzerland.

8. This project, 'Changing Direction', organised by Alison Pritchard and myself, led to an international seminar at Hawkwood College, Stroud, in 1979. Sponsors were: Continuing Management Education Programme, Loughborough University of Technology; Gatsby Charitable Foundation, London; Intermediate Technology Development Group, London; International Foundation for Social Innovation, Paris; Joseph Rowntree Charitable Trust, York; Scott Bader Commonwealth, Northamptonshire; Vanier Institute of the Family, Ottawa.

9. 'The Redistribution Of Work' (available from Turning Point, see 2) was written in 1981, following two Turning Point meetings on this subject. It includes short summaries of talks by Professor Charles Handy (then Warden of St. George's House, Windsor) on the future of work and by Sheila Rothwell (Director of Employment Studies, Administrative Staff College, Henley) on women's work and men's work.

10. Michael Marien: 'Societal Directions And Alternatives', 1976. Marien, the outstanding bibliographer of futures literature, has subsequently edited *Future Survey* — now covering several thousand items — for the World Future Society, 4916 St. Elmo Avenue, Bethesda, MD 20814, U.S.A.

11. James Robertson: 'Power, Money And Sex: Towards A New Social Balance': Marion Boyars, 1976.

12. Willis W. Harman: 'An Incomplete Guide To The Future': Norton, 1979. Willis Harman is President of the Institute of Noetic Sciences.

13. In 'The Third Wave': Collins, 1980, Alvin Toffler moved noticeably away from the super-industrial vision of 'Future Shock': Bodley Head, 1970, towards a more humane vision of the future. Another best-selling American author, John Naisbitt, writing in 'Megatrends': Warner, 1982, about the 'new directions transforming our lives', included shifts from centralisation to decentralisation, from institutional help to self-help, from representative democracy to participatory democracy and from hierarchies to networking — all of which are characteristics of what I call the SHE future.

14. Robin Clarke: 'Notes For The Future': Thames and Hudson, 1975.

15. Dennis Meadows et al: 'The Limits To Growth': Universe Books, 1972.

16. M. Mesarovic and E. Pestel: 'Mankind At The Turning Point': Hutchinson, 1975.

17. Ronald Higgins: 'The Seventh Enemy: The Human Factor In The Global Crisis': Hodder and Stoughton, 1978.

18. Robert L. Heilbroner: 'An Inquiry Into The Human Prospect': Calder and Boyars, 1975.

19. The Ecologist: 'Blueprint For Survival': Penguin, 1972.

20. Conservation Society: Annual report for 1976: Conservation Society, 12A Guildford Street, Chertsey, Surrey KT16 8BR.

21. Two recent examples are: 'Last Aid: The Medical Dimensions Of Nuclear War' by International Physicians for the Prevention of Nuclear War: Freeman, 1982; Jim Garrison: 'From Hiroshima To Harrisburg; The Unholy Alliance': SCM Press, 1980.

22. Menard Press, 8 The Oaks, Woodside Avenue, London N12 8AR, have recently published many good pamphlets on this subject.

23. Herman E. Daly (ed.): 'Toward A Steady-State Economy': Freeman, San Francisco, 1973. A full account of Ophuls' thinking is in 'Ecology And The Politics Of Scarcity': Freeman, 1977.

24. Herman Kahn et al: 'The Next 200 Years': Associated Business Programmes, London, 1977.

25. Daniel Bell: 'The Coming Of Post-Industrial Society': Penguin, 1976.

26. Michael Marien: 'The Two Visions Of Post-Industrial Society': *Futures*, October 1977, pp. 415-431.

27. Robert L. Heilbroner: 'Business Civilisation In Decline': Marion Boyars, 1976.

28. William Irwin Thompson: 'Evil And World Order': Harper and Row, 1976.

29. L. S. Stavrianos: 'The Promise Of The Coming Dark Age': Freeman, 1976.

30. Murray Bookchin: 'Post-Scarcity Anarchism': Wildwood House, 1974.

31. R. H. Tawney: 'Religion And The Rise Of Capitalism': Penguin, 1938.

32. Gurth Higgin: 'Scarcity, Abundance And Depletion: The Challenge To Continuing Management Education': Inaugural Lecture, Loughborough University of Technology, 1975.

33. Axel Leijonhufvud: 'On Keynesian Economics And The Economics Of

Keynes': Oxford, 1968.

34. Future historians of ideas may look back on economics as a fairly short-lived structure of reasoning and speculation erected on the values of the industrial age. Alternatively, economists — like Mark Lutz and Kenneth Lux: 'The Challenge Of Humanistic Economics': Benjamin/Cummins, 1979, and Herman Daly: 'Steady State Economics', Freeman, 1977 — may find ways of extending their discipline to embrace the needs of social justice, the ecosystem and real people (as contrasted with homo economicus). See also 'Human Economy: A Bibliography', published by the Human Economy Center, c/o Don Stone, Dept. of Accounting, School of Business Administration, University of Massachusetts, Amherst, Mass. 01003, U.S.A.

35. Edith Simon: 'The Saints', Penguin, 1972.

36. Books contributing to the new world-view include: Gregory Bateson: 'Mind And Nature: A Necessary Unity': Wildwood House, 1979; Fritjof Capra: 'The Turning Point': Wildwood House, 1982; Marilyn Ferguson: 'The Aquarian Conspiracy: Personal And Social Transformation In The 1980s': Tarcher, 1980; J. E. Lovelock: 'Gaia: A New Look At Life On Earth': OUP, 1979; Jeremy Rifkin: 'Entropy': Viking Press, 1980; Theodore Roszak: 'Person/Planet: The Creative Disintegration Of Industrial Society': Anchor Doubleday, 1978; Peter Russell: 'The Awakening Earth: Our Next Evolutionary Leap': RKP, 1982.

Also recommended: John Lane: 'The Death And Resurrection Of The Arts": Green Alliance, 60 Chandos Place, London WC2, 1982.

37. Martin Pfaff (ed.): 'Frontiers Of Social Thought': North Holland, 1976.

38. Fred Hirsch: 'Social Limits To Growth': RKP, 1977.

39. Hazel Henderson: 'Creating Alternative Futures: The End Of Economics': Berkley Windhover, 1978. In this and her later book "The Politics Of The Solar Age: Alternatives To Economics': Anchor Doubleday, 1981, Henderson has provided a powerful and influential critique of economics, and convincing pointers to an alternative future. Also see 34.

40. Peter Draper: 'The Unhealthy Economy: A Physician's View': *The Lancet,* October 30, 1976. Dr. Draper is director of the Unit for the Study of Health Policy, 8 Newcomen Street, London SE1 1YR. The Unit's publications have included: 'Health, The Mass Media, And The National Health Service', 1977; 'The NHS In The Next 30 years', 1978; and 'Rethinking Community Medicine', 1979.

41. Hugh Stretton: 'Housing And Government': Australian Broadcasting Commission, Sydney, 1974.

42. E. F. Schumacher, 'Small Is Beautiful: Economics As If People Mattered': first published by Blond and Briggs, 1973, has probably provided the most influential introduction to what I call the SHE economic path. 'Small Is Beautiful', together with Schumacher's subsequent books, 'A Guide For The Perplexed': Cape, 1977, and 'Good Work': Cape, 1979, and his work with the Intermediate Technology Development Group, the Scott Bader Commonwealth and the Soil Association, established him as one of the most widely known and effective pioneers of a future as if people matter. Schumacher Societies have been set up in England (c/o Satish Kumar, Ford House, Hartland, Devon) and in the U.S.A. (c/o Robert Swann, Box 76, RD3 Great Barrington, MA 01230).

43. Duane Elgin: 'Voluntary Simplicity: Towards A Way Of Life That Is Outwardly Simple, Inwardly Rich': Morrow, 1981. Among Elgin's sources is the Values and Lifestyles Program of SRI International, the prestigious business research institute in California which has documented the shift in American values from outer-directedness to inner-directedness.

44. Tom Forrester: 'Do The British Sincerely Want To Be Rich?': *New Society*, April 28, 1977.

45. The literature on a more conserving use of resources is now very large. It includes: Amory Lovins: 'Soft Energy Paths': Penguin, 1977; Barbara Ward: 'Progress For A Small Planet': Norton, 1979; Kimon Valaskakis and others: 'The Conserver Society': Harper and Row, 1979; Lester Brown: 'Building A Sustainable Society': Norton, 1981; 'Quarry Australia?': (eds.) Birrell, Hill and Stanley: OUP, 1982. Effective pleas for farming as a biological activity, not a mechanical one, include: Marion Shoard: 'The Theft Of The Countryside': Temple Smith, 1980; Robert Waller: 'The Agricultural Balance Sheet': Green Alliance — see 36.

46. John Davis: 'Technology For A Changing World': Intermediate Technology Publications, 1979.

47. Abraham H. Maslow: 'Motivation And Personality': 2nd edition, Harper and Row, 1970.

48. The literature relevant to a people-centred future ranges very widely, as three examples will show. Mike Cooley: 'Architect Or Bee? The Human Technology Relationship': Langley Technical Services, 1979, argues that new technology should be used to create a world in which human beings may fully develop and in which production will be socially useful. John Rowan: 'Ordinary Ecstasy': RKP, 1976, describes the person-centred approach of humanistic psychology. Paolo Freire, for example in 'Pedagogy Of The Oppressed': Penguin, 1972, describes education as the practice of freedom in which men and women discover how to participate in the transformation of their world.

49. George McRobie: 'Small Is Possible': Cape, 1981, contains a wealth of information on small scale self-reliance. George McRobie worked with E. F. Schumacher (see 42) and, after Schumacher's death, succeeded him as chairman of the Intermediate Technology Development Group.

On food, see: Colin Tudge: 'The Famine Business': Penguin, 1979; Patrick and Shirley Rivers: 'Diet For A Small Island': Turnstone, 1981; Joan Dye Gussow: 'The Feeding Web: Issues In Nutritional Ecology': Bull, California, 1978.

50. Leopold Kohr: 'The Breakdown Of Nations': Dutton (1978 edition); Kirkpatrick Sale: 'Human Scale': Secker and Warburg, 1980. Stan Windass: 'Local Initiatives In Great Britain': Foundation for Alternatives, The

Rookery, Adderbury, Banbury, Oxon, gives profiles of local enterprise trusts, community co-operatives, and other local economic initiatives. Alan Bollard: 'Small Beginnings: Prospect For A New Industrial Path', 1983, is the seventh of a series of reports from the Intermediate Technology Development Group (see 5) on an 'Alternative Industrial Framework For The U.K.'. Sudbury 2001 (67 Elm Street East, Sudbury, Ontario, Canada P3E 4S7): 'Retrospect: Prospect': January, 1981, describes a strategy for regional self-reliance and relative self-sufficiency. Decentralisation of today's mass media will go with decentralisation of government and the economy. That is an aim of Community Communications (Simon Partridge, 92 Huddleston Road, London N7).

51. 'North South: A Programme For Survival" (The Brandt Report): Pan, 1980, spelled out a progressive approach to third world development, fatally weakened, however, by the emphasis which it gave to the need to revive economic growth in the rich countries. Edgar Owens and Robert Shaw: 'Development Reconsidered': Heath, 1972, was an early plea for a new approach to third world development. 'What Now: Another Development' was published in *Development Dialogue,* July 1975, and was followed up by Marc Nerfin (ed.): 'Another Development: Approaches And Strategies': 1977, both published by the Dag Hammarskjold Foundation, Uppsala, Sweden. The implications of 'another development' both for third world countries and for the world economy can be studied in subsequent issues of *Development Dialogue,* and in the IFDA Dossiers published by the International Foundation for Development Alternatives, Nyon, Switzerland. 'Another development' for third world countries and the SHE development path for industrialised countries are both parallel and complementary. See 7. Also Nordal Akerman: 'Can Sweden Be Shrunk?' in *Development Dialogue,* 1979:2. I am grateful to David Radcliffe of the Faculty of Education, University of Western Ontario, for pointing out the similarities between the SHE development path and the Gandhian concept of Sarvodaya — see Detlef Kantowsky: Sarvodaya: The Other Development': Vikas, New Delhi, 1980. Also see: Frances Moore Lappé and Joseph Collins: 'Food First: Beyond The Myth Of Scarcity': Ballantyne, 1979.

52. Many relevant publications include: David Dickson: 'Alternative Technology And The Politics Of Technical Change': Fontana, 1974; Valentina Borremans: 'Reference Guide To Convivial Tools': (Apdo 479, Cuernavaca, Mexico); John Todd and Nancy Jack Todd: 'Tomorrow Is Our Permanent Address': Harper and Row, 1980; TRANET Newsletter (Transnational Network on Alternative Technology, P.O. Box 567, Rangeley, ME 04970, U.S.A.). Relevant organisations include: Intermediate Technology Development Group (Chairman: George McRobie; U.S. Chairman: Ward Morehouse) — also see 5, 46 and 49; Centre for Alternative Technology, Machynlleth, Wales; NATTA (Network for Alternative Technology and Technology Assessment), Open University, Milton Keynes; CAITS (Centre for Alternative Industrial and Technological

Systems), North East London Polytechnic.

53. *Built Environment,* Vol. 4, No. 4, 1978, on 'A Choice Of Futures' and Vol. 5, No. 3, 1979, on 'New Faces, New Places', both edited by Tom Hancock, are relevant. Two organisations concerned with these issues are: The Town and Country Planning Association, 17 Carlton House, Terrace, London SW1; URBED (Urban and Economic Development), 359 The Strand, London WC2. Wider access to land may require changes in tenure and ownership. For background see Richard Norton-Taylor: 'Whose Land Is It Anyway?': Turnstone, 1982.

54. See 43 and 44.

55. The significance of the fact that industrialised countries, as well as third world countries, have dual economies comprising a formal and an informal part, first occurred to me when I read Peter Cadogan's discussion of the 'gift economy' in his pamphlet 'Direct Democracy': 1 Hampstead Hill Gardens, London NW3, 1975. The dual economy then provided the focus for my paper 'Towards Post-Industrial Liberation And Reconstruction', at the annual meeting of the British Association for the Advancement of Science at Aston University in summer 1977 (later published in New Universities Quarterly, Vol. 32, No. 1, Winter 1977/78). Many other people in various countries were developing a similar approach around the same time. For example: Scott Burns: 'The Household Economy': Beacon, 1975; Hazel Henderson's chapter on 'The Emerging Counter-Economy' in 'Creating Alternative Futures' (see 39); Jonathan Gershuny: 'After Industrial Society: The Emerging Self-Service Economy': Macmillan, 1978; Joseph Huber (ed.): 'Anders Arbeiten — Anders Wirtschaften'; Fischer Alternativ, Frankfurt, 1979; Graeme Shankland: 'Our Secret Economy': The Response Of The Informal Economy To The Rise Of Mass Unemployment': Anglo-German Foundation, London, 1980. Throughout these years, Bill Dyson and his colleagues at the Vanier Institute of the Family, Ottawa, have done pioneering work on informal economic activities as an aspect of a more familial society.

56. S. J. Prais: 'The Evolution Of Giant Firms In Britain': Cambridge University Press, 1976.

57. Report No. 2 of the Royal Commission on the 'Distribution Of Income And Wealth' under Lord Diamond's chairmanship: HMSO, Cmnd. 6172, 1975.

58. George C. Lodge: 'The New American Ideology': Knopf, 1976.

59. James Robertson: 'Profit Or People? The New Social Role Of Money': Calder and Boyars, 1974.

I was grateful to Peter Wilsher (Sunday Times) and Maurice Goldsmith (Science Policy Foundation) for jointly organising a conference in the Festival Hall in 1974 to discuss these ideas, and to Peter McGregor (Anglo-German Foundation for the Study of Industrial Society) for supporting a subsequent project on the legal and financial structure of enterprises.

Peter Jay: 'Employment, Inflation And Politics': Institute of Economic Affairs, Occasional Paper 41, London, 1976, recommended a market economy in which enterprises are owned and controlled by their workers.

Folkert Wilken: 'The Liberation Of Capital': Allen and Unwin, 1982, provides a fundamental analysis of co-operation as an alternative form of economic organisation to both capitalism and communism.

60. Report of the Committee of Enquiry under Lord Bullock's chairmanship on 'Industrial Democracy': HMSO, Cmnd. 6706, 1977.

61. Louis O. Kelso and Patricia Hetter: 'Two Factor Theory: The Economics Of Reality': Random House, 1967.

Shann Turnbull; 'New Money Sources And Profit Motives': Company Directors Association of Australia, 1975.

Turnbull has recently collaborated with Robert Swann — see 42 — on the development of new forms of currency, including local currencies backed by local commodities such as timber, as an aspect of decentralisation — following ideas explored by Ralph Borsodi and Mildred Loomis (School of Living, Deep Run Farm, RD7 York, PA 17402, USA).

62. Peter Drucker: 'The Unseen Revolution: How Pension Fund Socialism Came To America': Harper and Row, 1976.

63. C.A.R. Crosland: 'The Future Of Socialism' Cape, 1956.

64. 'Time To Care': 1982, one of many valuable reports from the Swedish Government's Secretariat For Future Studies, Stockholm, is a perceptive diagnosis by an official body of the present crisis of the Welfare State.

Ivan Illich: 'Medical Nemesis': Calder and Boyars, 1975, probably provides the most influential critique of formal medicine in recent years.

The European Region of the World Health Organisation (Copenhagen), in a current series of papers on health education, healthy lifestyles and self-help in health, is making an important contribution to a new social paradigm of health.

Brian Inglis: 'Natural Medicine': Collins, 1979, provides an introduction to alternative therapies.

Three organisations active in this field are: The Scientific and Medical Network (George Blaker, Lake House, Ockley, Nr. Dorking, Surrey RH5 5NS); The Association for New Approaches to Cancer (Marcus McCausland, 1a Addison Crescent, London W14 8JP); The Cancer Help Centre (Dr. Alec Forbes, 7 Downfield Road, Clifton, Bristol BS8 2TG).

Important contributions to thinking in this field have been made by John McKnight (Centre for Urban Affairs, Northwestern University, Illinois), and Trevor Hancock (Toronto Department of Health). Valuable publications include Alex Scott-Samuel's journal *Radical Community Medicine* (5 Lyndon Drive, Liverpool); and 'Health Care: Three Reports From 2030A.D.' from Trend Analysis Program, American Council of Life Insurance, TAP No. 19, Spring, 1980.

Also see 4, 40 and 'The Aquarian Conspiracy' (see 36) for some of the many other relevant publications.

65. For example, J. K. Galbraith: 'The New Industrial State': Pelican, 1969.

66. Norman Macrae: 'The Coming Entrepreneurial Revolution': *The Economist,* December 25, 1976.

67. T. S. Kuhn: 'The Structure Of Scientific Revolutions': University of Chicago Press, 1970.

68. Boston Women's Health Book Collective: 'Our Bodies Ourselves': Simon and Schuster, 1976.

69. Ciaran McKeown: 'The Price Of Peace': Belfast, 1976.

70. Jim Cairns: 'The Quiet Revolution': Widescope, 1975 and 'Growth To Freedom': Down To Earth Foundation, Canberra, 1979.

71. Aurelio Peccei: 'The Human Quality': Pergamon, 1977.

72. Gail Stewart and Cathy Starrs: 'Reworking The World: A Report On Changing Concepts Of Work': Ottawa, 1973.

73. For example, Clive Jenkins and Barrie Sherman: 'The Collapse Of Work': Eyre Methuen, 1979, and 'The Leisure Shock': Eyre Metheun, 1981.

74. David Elliott: 'The Future Of Work': Open University Press, 1975. David Elliott and Ruth Elliott: 'The Control Of Technology': Wykeham Publications, 1976.

75. William Morris: 'Selected Writings And Designs' (ed.) Asa Briggs. Penguin, 1962, pp. 118, 119.

76. The volume of relevant publications is vast and growing daily. Useful references are included in the Turning Point paper on 'The Redistribution Of Work' — see 9. For the bottom-up approach the following are also valuable: BURN (British Unemployment Resources Network) Newsletter, c/o Birmingham Settlement, 318 Summer Lane, Birmingham B19 6RL; Guy Dauncey: 'Nice Work If You Can Get It': National Extension College, Cambridge, 1983; 'Community Business Works': Report from the Gulbenkian Foundation, London, 1982.

77. The future of leisure is linked with the future of work. Leisure activities may involve: spending money (e.g. going to the theatre); not spending, nor saving, nor earning, money (e.g. walking, reading books from the public library); saving money (e.g. DIY): earning money from hobbies (e.g. photography). Money-saving and money-earning leisure often becomes indistinguishable from work. So does what sociologists call 'essential activities', such as housework and childcare.

W. H. Martin and S. Mason: 'Leisure And Work: The Choices For 1991 And 2001': Leisure Consultants, 1982, provides a good overview for readers from businesses and other organisations.

Recent conference proceedings from the Leisure Studies Association are useful, e.g. on 'Work And Leisure: The Implications Of Technological Change': Tourism and Recreational Research Unit, Edinburgh, 1982.

78. Many new initiatives in education are springing up which point in the right direction, including 'education otherwise', 'education with production', 'education for capability'. Also education for co-operative self-reliance, person-centred education, education for international understanding and peace, and education for conservation.

The new paradigm of education and learning has still to crystallise. However, see: James Hemming: 'The Betrayal Of Youth: Secondary Education Must Be Changed': Marion Boyars, 1980.

The Dartington annual conferences (Dartington Hall, Totnes, Devon) on 'new themes in education' provide a valuable forum.

79. A good account of this proposal is Keith Roberts: 'Automation, Unemployment And The Distribution Of Income': European Centre for Work and Society, Maastricht, Netherlands, 1982. 'Work And Employment In Post-Manufacturing Society', by the well-known British economic commentator Michael Shanks, is another valuable paper from the Centre — which also publishes a very useful newsletter.

80. The Corn Laws were not repealed until 1846, only five years before the Great Exhibition of 1851 which is now regarded as marking the peak of Britain's industrial supremacy. This is a good instance of a general rule: governments cannot be expected to initiate social change; they have to be pressed hard to remove obstacles to social change which they themselves impose.

81. Gregory Bateson: 'Steps To An Ecology Of Mind': Paladin, 1973.

82. Raimundo Panikkar: 'Myth In Religious Phenomenology': Monchanin, Montreal, June/December, 1975.

83. Ivan Illich: 'Tools For Conviviality': Calder and Boyars, 1973.

84. 'The Serving Professions?': Vanier Institute of the Family, Ottawa, 1974.

85. John Southgate and Rosemary Randall: 'The Barefoot Psychoanalyst': Association of Karen Horney Psychoanalytic Counsellors, 1976.

86. Various publications from the Manager (Public Affairs), Royal Bank of Canada, Montreal.

87. John Turner: 'Housing By People': Marion Boyars, 1976. Also see: Sarah Eno and Dave Treanor: 'The Collective Housing Handbook': Laurieston Hall, Castle Douglas, Kirkcudbrightshire, Scotland, 1982.

88. Alice Coleman: 'Is Planning Really Necessary?: Royal Geographical Society, London, May 1976.

89. John Adams: 'Transport Planning: Vision and Practice': RKP, 1981.

90. Abraham Maslow: 'Towards A Psychology Of Being': Van Nostrand Reinhold, 1968.

91. Sir James Robertson: 'Transition In Africa': Hurst, 1974.

92. Peter Mathias: 'The First Industrial Nation': Methuen, 1969.

Good accounts of the social processes involved in the industrial revolution are in: Karl Polanyi: 'The Great Transformation: The Political And Economic Origins Of Our Time': Beacon, 1957; Harold Perkin: 'The Origins Of Modern English Society, 1780-1880': RKP, 1969.

93. The importance of networking, as a form of social activism based on informal contact between persons as contrasted with formal relations between organisations, has become widely recognised in the last five years. See: Byron Kennard: 'Nothing Can Be Done: Everything Is Possible': Brick House, 1982; Jessica Lipnack and Jeffrey Stamps: 'Networking': Doubleday, 1982;

Two very different examples of networks in Britain today are the Lifestyle Movement (Horace Dammers, Dean of Bristol, The Cathedral, Bristol BS1 5TJ) and the Futures Network (12 Wentworth Court, Brighouse, West Yorks HD6 3XD).

94. Stephen Verney: 'Into The New Age': Fontana, 1976.

95. Gurth Higgin: 'Symptoms Of Tomorrow': Plume Press/Ward Lock, 1973.

96. Eric Berne: 'Games People Play': Grove Press, 1964.

97. Michael Maccoby: 'The Gamesman': Simon and Schuster, 1976.

98. Recent publications from the Association for Humanistic Psychology, 325 9th Street, San Francisco, CA 94103, USA, have been concerned with the links between personal change and social change. See also John Rowan (48).

99. The following books provide relevant background to this chapter: Erik Damman: 'The Future In Our Hands': Pergamon, 1979; Tony Gibson: 'People Power': Penguin, 1979; Charles Hampden-Turner: 'Radical Man: The Process Of Psycho-Social Development': Doubleday, 1970; Robert Jungk: 'The Everyman Project': Thames and Hudson, 1976; Bruce Stokes: 'Helping Ourselves': Norton, 1981; Robert Theobald: 'Beyond Despair: Directions For America's Third Century': New Republic, 1976.

One of many movements and initiatives for a better future and a better world, which helps to convey the range of activities with which this chapter is concerned, is the Right Livelihood Foundation (Jacob von Uexkull, Oncham, Isle of Man). The Foundation has awarded Alternative Nobel Prizes, as follows:

1980 Stephen Gaskin, Plenty (international relief, USA)
     Hassan Fathy, International Institute for Appropriate Technology (Egypt)
1981 Mike Cooley, Lucas Aerospace (socially useful production, Britain)
     Bill Mollison, Permaculture (Australia)
     Patrick van Rensburg, Education with Production (Botswana)
1982 Petra Kelly, Green Party (Germany)
     Anwar Fazal, International Consumer Unions (Malaysia)
     Sir George Trevelyan, Wrekin Trust (Britain)
     Participatory Institute for Development Alternatives (Sri Lanka).

100. Charles Hampden-Turner: 'Sane Asylum': Morrow, 1977.

101. Peter Abbs and Graham Carey: 'Proposals For A New College': Heinemann Educational Books, 1977.

102. Elizabeth Dodson Gray: 'Patriarchy As A Conceptual Trap': Roundtable Press, 1982. Rosemary Ruether: 'New Woman, New Earth':

Seabury, 1975. Henryk Skolimowski: 'Eco-Philosophy': Marion Boyars, 1981.

103. The following books point towards new political theories and strategies which are, to a greater or lesser extent, in keeping with the polycentric, people-centred approach: Dennis Altman: 'Rehearsals For Change': Fontana, 1979 (Australia); Junie Morosi: 'Sex, Prejudice And Politics': Widescope, 1975 (Australia); Sheila Rowbotham, Lynne Segal, Hilary Wainwright: 'Beyond The Fragments: Feminism And The Making Of Socialism': Merlin, 1979 (Britain); Neils Meyer, Helveg Petersen, Villy Sorensen: 'Revolt From The Centre': Marion Boyars, 1981 (Denmark); Roger Garaudy: 'The Alternative Future: A Vision Of Christian Marxism': Penguin, 1976 (France); André Gorz: 'Ecology As Politics': Pluto Press, 1975 (France); Clement Bezold: 'Anticipatory Democracy: People In The Politics Of The Future': Random House, 1978 (USA); Mark Satin: 'New Age Politics: Healing Self and Society': Dell, 1979 (USA).

The following initiatives and movements are among those which have, broadly, taken this approach: Fourth World (John Papworth, Britain); Revolt from the Centre (Meyer, Petersen and Sorensen, Denmark); The Future In Our Hands (Erik Damman, Norway); New Age Alliance (Mark Satin, USA); Planetary Initiatives (Donald Keys, USA).

104. Karl Marx: 'The Poverty of Philosophy'.

105. The conventional reformist approach to social change goes with representative democracy; the polycentric approach to social change goes with participatory democracy. C.M. Macpherson: 'The Life And Times Of Liberal Democracy': OUP, 1977, provides interesting and lucid background.

The question often arises whether to work for a SHE future through the existing processes of representative politics. In Britain, the Ecology Party and groups in other political parties like SERA (Socialist Environment and Resources Association) and the Liberal Ecology Group, have been doing good work — as, more conspicuously, have the Greens in Germany. On the other hand, it can be argued that the competitive processes of parliamentary and electoral politics have now become self-stultifying to the point where more can probably be achieved by disengaging from them and working outside them — in ways which may in due course help to influence politicians of all persuasions.

The question will remain open, the choice of where to commit one's energies to the processes of change being one for each person to decide.

106. I am grateful to Tom Kitwood, School of Science and Society, Bradford University for putting this point to me so clearly. Also to Krishan Kumar, whose 'Prophecy And Progress: The Sociology Of Industrial And Post-Industrial Society': Penguin, 1978, contains valuable background to this and related issues.

107. I was given opportunities to articulate 'a post-Marxist strategy for the post-industrial revolution' at two conferences in 1978. One, on 'Shaping The Future: Canada In A Global Society', was organised by Walter Baker of the

Ottawa Centre for Policy and Management Studies and his colleagues. The other, in Paris, on 'The Long-Term Future Of International Relations', was organised by Hugues de Jouvenel and his colleagues at Futuribles.

The literature on Marxism is, of course, immense. A relevant summary is in A.S. Cohan: 'Theories of Revolution': Nelson, London, 1975. Leszek Kolakowski's three-volume 'Main Currents Of Marxism': OUP, 1978, is one of the most comprehensive and authoritative accounts of Marxism. Ernst Fischer: 'Marx In His Own Words': Penguin, 1973, is also useful.

108. Karl Marx: 'Preface To A Contribution To A Critique Of Political Economy'.

109. Stafford Beer: 'Designing Freedom': John Wiley, 1974.

110. Donald Schon: 'Beyond The Stable State': Penguin, London, 1973.

111. The non-violent anarchist tradition of Tolstoy, Kropotkin and Gandhi has been at odds with the organising tendencies and assumptions of industrialised society. It is likely to attract growing mainstream interest, as the post-industrial revolution gathers pace. For an introduction, see for example: Colin Ward: 'Anarchy In Action': George Allen and Unwin; George Woodcock (ed.): 'The Anarchist Reader': Fontana, 1977; George Woodcock: 'Gandhi': Fontana, 1972.

112. One example is East/West Peace People (Peter Cadogan, 1 Hampstead Hill Gardens, London NW3). Another is Dunamis, St. James Church, 197 Piccadilly, London W1, in which Ronald Higgins — see 17 — is a moving spirit. Dunamis is one of many interesting new initiatives encouraged by Rev. Donald Reeves at St. James, Piccadilly. It is linked with Commonwork and Centrespace, two neighbouring centres in Kent established by Jenifer and Neil Wates, Mark Collier, and their colleagues.

113. This approach is treated at greater length in my article 'The Future of Work: The Roles Of Men And Women In The Transition To A SHE Future': *Women's Studies International Quarterly,* Vol. 4, No. 1, Special Issue on 'Women In Futures Research'.

Two useful books are: Birgitta Wistrand: 'Swedish Women On The Move': The Swedish Insititute, 1981. Virginia Novarra: 'Women's Work, Men's Work: The Ambivalence of Equality', Marion Boyars, 1980.

INDEX

149

151

152

153

154

155